DANCE

'. . . Young people are realising that modern dance is exciting, challenging and relevant to *them*.'

Arlene Phillips

Modern dance is no longer something to be enjoyed by the 'privileged' few, but most fans will enjoy reading more about it. Ian Woodward traces the history of modern dance from its origins early this century – the pioneers, founders, and the major influences in its development from classical ballet. He explains how a modern dance is created and choreographed, and explores the directions dance may take in the future. There's also an information section about dancers, choreographers and dances to see, lists of modern dance schools and companies, and ideas for further reading.

Packed with fascinating facts, this is essential reading for anyone who is interested in modern dance.

ABOUT THE AUTHOR

Ian Woodward was born in the Welsh
cathedral town of Brecon and now lives with
his wife and two children in a Hertfordshire
village. He travels all over the world as a
writer specialising in theatre, films, television
and music, as well as dance. He is the author
of many books on subjects ranging from
clowns, music and wild life to monsters,
ponies and the supernatural, plus biographies
of movie stars Audrey Hepburn and Glenda
Jackson. With his wife, Zenka, he has edited
several poetry anthologies for young readers.
His numerous books on dance include
Balletgoing, *Ballet*, *Understanding Ballet*,
Ballet and the Dance, *Ballet* (Teach Yourself
Books), *Ballet Stories* and a companion to
this new book, *Spotlight on Ballet*.

Dance

Ian Woodward

KNIGHT BOOKS
Hodder and Stoughton

Copyright © Ian Woodward 1984
First published by Knight Books 1984

British Library C.I.P.
Woodward, Ian
   Dance
   1. Modern dance – Juvenile literature
   I. Title
   793.3′2   GV1783

   ISBN 0-340-32088-5

Printed and bound in Great Britain for Hodder and
Stoughton Paperbacks, a division of Hodder and
Stoughton Ltd., Mill Road, Dunton Green,
Sevenoaks, Kent (Editorial Office: 47 Bedford Square,
London, WC1 3DP) by Richard Clay (The Chaucer Press) Ltd.,
Bungay, Suffolk. Photoset by Rowland Phototypesetting Ltd.,
Bury St Edmunds, Suffolk.

Contents

Third Step: SHOW BUSINESS DANCING – AND THE FUTURE

Fourth Step: A GUIDE TO DANCES, PERFORMERS, CHOREOGRAPHERS, COMPANIES AND SCHOOLS

   (i) *Schools where modern dance is taught*
  (ii) *Modern dance companies*
 (iii) *Suggested reading*

Foreword

by
ARLENE PHILLIPS

Television, film and stage choreographer
and director of TV's Hot Gossip

Ian Woodward's many books on ballet have already proved him to be an informative, entertaining writer in a field which can very easily be boring to the beginner. Many ballet writers fall into the trap of simply 'preaching to the converted', whereas Mr Woodward's books are always a pleasure to read, both to the confirmed balletgoer and to the reader with perhaps only a small interest in ballet.

Now he has written DANCE, and what a wonderful job he has done! From my own experience in teaching, as well as from the sacks of mail my own Hot Gossip dancers receive, I know how great a need there is for a straightforward, well-written and informative book on modern dance.

At the moment, happily, we are living in the middle of an exciting 'dance explosion' in Britain. As a result, children and young people all over the country are wanting to see more, hear more, and find out more about modern dance.

It's certainly a bewildering subject, with dance groups, classes and choreographers all working away frantically, and there often seems to be as many styles of dance and definitions of styles as there are teachers. But this book, I am pleased to say, carefully and simply plots the history of modern dance, the resulting 'mainstreams' of styles and techniques – and also includes essential information from choreographers and dancers working in the extremely demanding world of dance companies, as well as the commercial worlds of television and cabaret.

I think it's worth mentioning that, just as a few years ago the big breakthrough for a modern dance company was to fill a theatre such as Sadler's Wells, the biggest breakthrough for dancers in recent years has been that dance groups are now featured in their own right on television shows, instead of being just a bunch of anonymous bodies bouncing away in the background behind a singer.

All over the country young people are realising that modern dance is exciting, challenging and relevant to them, no longer something to be appreciated only by a knowledgeable, 'privileged' elite.

The time has come for us now to start to reap the benefit of all this energy and hard work . . . but, sadly, although there are now many more classes for young people to attend, and some schools are at last making dance a part of their regular curriculum, there are still nowhere near enough outlets for all this talent. We need more halls and theatres, and more companies to fill those halls and theatres.

In the United States, there are new companies and smaller groups continually developing and finding support, not to mention the fine old pioneers who are still thriving and inspiring us all – including my personal all-time favourite, Alvin Ailey – but in this country we have a long way to go before we seriously rival the growing opportunities now available to young dancers in America.

But I am optimistic about the future and thrilled to see how the role of dance is changing and growing. I can't wait to welcome the developments of the next few years.

Meanwhile, to all those who want to dance – work hard; and to all the many lovers of dance – *enjoy*!

Arlene Phillips

First Step

MODERN DANCE BACKGROUND

Chapter 1

THE APPEAL OF MODERN DANCE

The American modern dancer and choreographer Gloria Newman likes to tell the story of the young man named Ted who, after seeing a performance by her company, went backstage afterwards to say how much he had enjoyed the show. It was the first time he had seen dance 'live' on stage.

'Terrific!' exclaimed nineteen-year-old Ted. 'I dig what you're doing. I wish everybody had been here. Why can't we have this all the time? Every place. Like sports.'

'I wish we *could* make dance as popular as sports,' the choreographer replied. She felt the warm rush of Ted's enthusiasm, and so responded at once with her own.

'In sports you have action . . . plotted movement . . . opposing forces fighting for the same thing. In dance we have action . . . plotted movement . . . a confrontation. And besides,' she smiled, 'we even have pretty girls.'

Ted, an enthusiast of baseball and football, nodded his appreciation of the pretty girls. Above all, he was convinced that dance and sport have so much in common the wonder was that he had not seen and appreciated a modern-dance performance earlier.

He knew for certain he was going to see modern dance again.

In the following pages I shall be examining many other dance forms which, in common with the technique enjoyed by Ted, fall outside the area of classical ballet. Tap and jazz dancing will be covered, as well as the pop-style dancing to be seen on television variety shows and in pantomimes, night clubs, musicals and summer shows.

It is all, by definition, *modern dance*.

No need for words

Some scientists who make a special study of mankind believe that dance is the oldest form of communication. They say it came even before speech. And it is this timelessness which a great deal of modern dance somehow conveys.

Robin Howard, the hotel and restaurant owner who founded the London Contemporary Dance Theatre in 1966, says: 'I believe modern dance is essentially timeless because it is always so firmly based on human beings as they are *today*.'

After seeing a performance of the New York company of Martha Graham, the most influential of all modern-style choreographers, a psychologist remarked: 'Her dances speak directly of human emotions without the need for words.'

This is probably because modern dance, and especially the far-reaching style invented by Miss Graham, represents a determined return to the body as the source of power and movement. From the *body* comes the impulse to movement . . . not from the *mind*, as so often seems to be the case in classical ballet.

Harmony of the body

Brigitte Lefevre, a former principal ballerina of the Paris Opéra Ballet, in 1972 formed the popular Ballet Théâtre du Silence, a modern dance company from France which London audiences saw for the first time in 1981. She now choreographs and dances with her company, and is also its director.

'In modern ballet,' she explains, 'we are trying to reach a wider public. Modern dance is more a question of harmony with one's own body than classical ballet, which is more codified and demands special actions. It also demands things you must not do, even if your body can do them.'

At this point Miss Lefevre stretches out her arms and bends her fingers upwards in an almost double-jointed movement.

'"No, no, Brigitte," my teacher always said. "You must not do that – it is not *classical*."'

Technique and motivation

The point about modern dance, the thing which makes it so different from classical ballet, is that it uses a freer style of movement. There are as many styles as there are choreographers. In ballet the style remains virtually the same, no matter how many choreographers create new works for it.

In ballet, therefore, the constant factor is *technique*. In modern dance it is *motivation* – the inner desire to make the movement – and the style used will stem entirely from the whim, personality, talent and mood of the choreographer.

Everything which is made – a bridge, a curtain, a work of art – is an image of its own time. As far as today's modern dance is concerned, the most dramatic image is surely the engine: restless, vibrating, compact, and technical. And as far as yesterday's classic dance is concerned, the strongest image is surely the swan: graceful, flowing, royal, and serene.

So modern dance stands for *energy*, classical ballet for *serenity*.

Two different worlds

Modern dance is everything classical ballet is not. One worships the floor, the other the air. One stresses weight, the other weightlessness. One favours the liberation of bare feet, the other the formality of shoes.

Classical ballet and modern dance – they are two different worlds. Some dancers discover during the course of their training, or perhaps their working life, that they are not suited to either of these worlds.

Many abandon ballet for modern dance. Lenny Westerdijk is such a person.

Miss Westerdijk is a Dutch dancer and choreographer now working in Britain. She began her career dancing with a classical ballet company, but was later disillusioned by that world and subsequently joined the modern-style Nederlands Dans Theater and Britain's Ballet Rambert before turning her hand to choreography and teaching.

She recalls why, as a young dancer, she eventually grew fed up with dancing extracts from ballets like *Swan Lake*, *Giselle* and *The Sleeping Beauty*. Her experience of the classics began to depress her.

'I never liked to stand in a line with a lot of other people,' she says, 'and I never enjoyed wearing a tutu; it seemed to me a bizarre way of dressing, one that had nothing to do with the real world.'

She found what she was looking for in modern dance. She is now rehearsal director of the London Contemporary Dance Theatre.

The roots of modern dance

The seed for the entertainment known as modern (or contemporary) dance was sown in the United States (and to a certain extent in Germany) during the first quarter of the twentieth century and began to sprout between 1926 and 1928. During these years Martha Graham gave her first solo concert and the important dancers Doris Humphrey and Charles Weidman staged performances together for the first time.

Two years later, in 1930, Germany's most exciting modern-dance creator, Mary Wigman, made her début in the USA. She influenced a great many people. One of her pupils, Hanya Holm, who accompanied her to America, stayed behind to teach – and many of her pupils, in turn, were to become some of today's finest exponents of modern dance, such as Alwin Nikolais and Glen Tetley.

Since so much modern dance as we now recognise it has been influenced by the legendary trio of Graham,

Humphrey and Weidman, and since all three performers came from the Denishawn school formed in Los Angeles in 1915 by American dance pioneers Ruth St Denis and Ted Shawn, their common training-ground has been called, appropriately, 'the cradle of American modern dance'.

The term 'modern dance' is commonly used to describe the type of dancing for which training in the Graham technique prepares a dancer: that is, a form of movement which relies to a great extent on the contraction and release of the body. But, as seen earlier, there are as many variations of the so-called 'modern dance technique' as there are people teaching it. The technique evolved by Humphrey and Weidman, for instance, depends largely on fall and recovery.

Definitions

Probably the biggest problem with modern dance, especially in Britain, is its name. The public is rightly confused as to what it is exactly, confused about whether it is something abstract or literal, confused about whether it deals with ideas or stories – or, indeed, whether it deals with anything.

Robert Cohan, the American-born former artistic director of the London Contemporary Dance Theatre, has always believed in the philosophy: 'Come and see us and you'll understand and enjoy.'

In the late 1960s, the American dancer and choreographer Alvin Ailey took his modern dance company on a tour of the Soviet Union. In Leningrad, home of the Kirov Ballet, he invited professional dancers to watch his company take class in the Graham technique.

'The first day,' explains Ailey, 'about three dancers came along. After that, about a hundred and fifty. They really flipped; they had never seen anything like it before.'

They saw – and understood.

So it's a case of not worrying too much about what modern dance *means* as whether, once seen, you like or dislike it.

Until the early 1970s, as a matter of fact, only a small and specialised audience existed for modern dance. It tended to take itself very seriously indeed . . . and it had great difficulty in saying exactly what it meant by 'modern' and sometimes what it meant by 'dance'.

Now all that has changed, even if definitions continue to be fuzzy. What is important is that the modern dance movement has created a big enough audience to fill a theatre such as, say, Sadler's Wells in London, or to attract the public in cities all over Britain to an annual six-week international festival of contemporary dance, known as Dance Umbrella.

An audience is sufficiently interested in modern dance, then, to fork out good money to see it. But what precisely is the fascination it holds for the dancers and choreographers who make it all happen?

'Why I perform modern dance'

Let us hear a few 'case histories'.

Australian dancer Barry Moreland, who choreographs dance works in both the classical and contemporary styles, explains: 'I'd been dancing classical ballet in Australia but I didn't much care for all those cardboard princes.

'A few years later, when working in West End musicals, I went to a matinée of the Martha Graham company. Graham was "saying" something interesting in movement, which is what dance is all about. The modern style fascinated me from that point on.'

Another dancer on whom Graham had such a big impact is the American Tim Wengerd.

He says: 'The Graham company was the only company I wanted to dance with – ever since I saw them one year in San Francisco. After that performance, I remember walking around the city until about four in the morning not really knowing who I was, or where I was, or what had happened to me.'

He is now a star of Graham's world-famous company in New York.

The Argentinian dancer, teacher and choreographer Noemi Lapzeson was also for many years a member of Graham's troupe, and of the London Contemporary Dance Theatre.

'When I first saw Martha Graham,' she reflects, 'I thought this woman was colossal. I stopped talking for two days. I was quite simply in a state of shock.'

Conversions

How and *why* do people become attracted to modern dance?

Micha Bergese at first trained as a 'cellist in his native Berlin.

Anthony van Laast, from England, was destined for a career in medicine, but gave it up when he faced the dissecting table.

Stephen Barker, an American, took a degree at university before pursuing a career in drama.

Ross McKim, who comes from Vancouver, previously played the clarinet and piano and conducted his school orchestra.

In later years, as ordinary theatregoers, they were attracted more to dancing than to their old studies, and so they changed courses – and went on to make their name in British modern dance. Van Laast, while working backstage at The Place, headquarters of the London Contemporary Dance Theatre and its School, used to watch what he describes as 'heavy' dance works and would think how *he* would have made them lighter and more humorous.

One day, quite by chance, Anthony van Laast discovered that he and Micha Bergese owned identical Suzuki motorbikes. Why not, they said, do a dance which started in the car park, with dancers forming groups in and around the parked cars, dancing to the combined sounds of electronic music and roaring, revving motor vehicles in the street?

It would mean that art would really imitate and reflect life. At the end of the piece, called *Outside-In*, the two boys would roar off on their motorbikes into the theatre proper, with the audience following.

Bergese, incidentally, abandoned the 'cello to become a contemporary-style dancer because, he felt, 'the expression of the body is so much wider than just a musical instrument'. McKim chose modern dance because he found it, quite simply, to be the best art form for communicating to others 'in a language we can all understand'. Barker felt the same thing.

Modern dance has *that* sort of power.

Chapter 2

HOW DIFFERENT IS DIFFERENT?

Most choreographers can work comfortably within only one style – in either classical or modern dance. A few, like the gifted American dance-maker Glen Tetley, have created their own approach or 'trade-mark', a sort of marriage between the opposing systems of classical and contemporary.

Even a versatile man of the theatre like Britain's Kenneth MacMillan, whose themes have been rather more 'modern' than most classical choreographers working today, admits that the modern style will never come naturally to him. He says: 'I've watched a lot of contemporary dance – I have a great admiration for Martha Graham – but I don't really have the right *feeling* in my body.'

In 1981, nevertheless, he created a full-length ballet all about the life of the legendary Isadora Duncan, the American dancer whose personality on stage influenced an entire generation. Modern dance's

Martha Graham and classical ballet's Frederick Ashton were equally touched by her artistry.

MacMillan's dance-drama, *Isadora*, created for the Royal Ballet company at Covent Garden, showed the dancing Duncan in bare feet, just as she had appeared in reality. Just before the production's première, MacMillan revealed: 'I'm attempting to bring ballet more into line with contemporary experiments in the arts.'

The ballerina Merle Park, who created the role in London, added at the time: 'After all the modern dance I have to do I'll be equipped to tackle anything. From now on you may find me rolling about on the floor, draped in polythene.'

She was referring, jokingly, to the sort of experimental modern dance where the performers are required to crawl around on the floor and make use of such 'odd' stage props as large paper bags, enormous inflated balloons and yards and yards of plastic sheeting.

Ancient and modern

Many people believe the differences in style and technique between classical and modern dance are so great that a dancer of one style should not attempt the style of another. Pearl Lang, for many years a star of the Martha Graham company, and a distinguished teacher and choreographer, is such a person.

'I believe,' says Miss Lang, 'that the trend of classical ballet companies to do modern dance is unfortunate. I find they take the visual, theatrical, surface qualities of the modern dance stage and superimpose them on ballet-trained bodies, so that moving in that particular way is no longer a living necessity but just a gimmicky decoration.'

She then explains: 'I'd rather see a ballet that makes use of its own language. That's beautiful. But when you find a ballet-trained body just turning the knee in and flexing the foot – well, that's not being modern. Movement must have its own reason for *being*.'

Features of modern dance

Many modern dance movements are done with the feet 'in parallel', or what classical dancers would call 'turned in'. The effect of this is that the top part of the body tends to sway sideways to balance leg extensions. It also accounts for the large number of semi-falling movements, and tilted balances, which are such a notable feature of American contemporary dance.

Someone going to a modern dance show for the first time – after, say, many visits to classical ballet – would also notice some other distinctive things about the way modern dancers use their bodies. The arm movements, for instance, are very often proudly curved, or gently flapped like the wings of a bird. There may be a loping kind of run, and lots of jumps.

Classical ballet, by contrast, is a matter of line and elegance and of standing on the toes. It's all to do with getting away from the earth, placing the dancer above, freeing herself or himself from gravity and becoming pure and elegant.

The spine in ballet dancers is held very straight: from the waist up it must all be cool and unruffled and exquisite. Most people in Britain and Western Europe have grown up with this image of ballet in front of them, of the beautiful ballerina and her handsome Prince Charming surrounded by an atmosphere of sweetness and light.

By contrast, modern dance starts from the earth, from the assumption that man stands on the earth – and so the spine should be like a snake. Ballet is all line; modern dance is all energy, and the line doesn't matter.

Paul Taylor, one of America's best-loved modern dancers, explains it like this: 'In ballet the restrictions are laid down and there's just one way to do it. Something is either ballet or not ballet. In modern dance you are free to make up your own rules. You are free to make your own restrictions. That is what modern dance is.'

The force of the earth

The Dutch dancer and choreographer Jaap Flier, who has been the head of such modern-style companies as the Nederlands Dance Theater and the Sydney Dance Theatre, adds: 'What I find so marvellous about the modern dance technique of somebody like Martha Graham is that although you are bound to the ground, her style uses the force of the earth to move up and away from it.

'They say that classical ballet does this too, but it doesn't; it only goes up. I think that the Graham technique, which is based so much on Oriental movement and philosophy, has evolved this way of going up in the mind and just staying on the ground with the body.'

Jaap Flier's old company, the Nederlands Dans Theater, was among the pioneers in the 1960s in helping to break down the barriers in Europe between classical and modern dance. Experiment and novelty has always been one of the hallmarks of this exciting company based in The Hague.

In other parts of the world, and notably in the United States, companies such as the Joffrey Ballet, American Ballet Theatre and the New York City Ballet were also introducing the modern idiom into some of their work. But the Dutch company insisted on training its dancers thoroughly in *both* forms, making available to the modern choreographer not only a new and exciting style but a style capable of doing justice to *all* types of dancing.

NDT dancers are taught never to indulge in difficult, 'flashy' steps simply for the sake of showing how technically talented they are – those leaps and bounds which, in classical ballet, are guaranteed to leave an audience gasping. The dancers are also told never to 'play' to the audience: the belief is that, in doing their own thing, the message will get across anyway.

The result is that these extremely versatile Dutch dancers do not perform modern dance like ballet dancers. Instead, they are sensitive to the special movement qualities of each work. They are not long-legged, rocketing child wonders, but mature and individual artists.

However, the London Contemporary Dance Theatre's great co-founder, Robert Cohan, offers a warning: 'There are some people who are semi-trained in ballet who think that although they can't make it in ballet they'll be able to make it in modern dance. Of course, this isn't true: they'll drop by the wayside in modern as well.

'I don't think the two things are comparable. I agree that there are two kinds of dance – good and bad – but there is also ballet dance and contemporary dance, and they are different styles and don't really mix too well.

'It's all right for dancers to have both trainings, but that's not to achieve a mixture: it's to achieve a refinement of your own particular training. I have rarely seen people who are good in both. Eventually they end up being good in one or the other.'

Rebels of the dance

It was in the United States, more than in any other country, where dancers felt a tremendous need to break away from the formal technique of classical ballet as performed in all the major capitals of the world. Yet what was it about ballet, exactly, which made all these people, the pioneers of modern dance, want to rebel?

This is what Paul Taylor told me: 'Quite simply, it's all due to the fact that it is very hard for American dancers and choreographers to get a feeling for the style of classical ballet, because it's based on court-liness, on a time which is not in our history.

'We're brought up as either Puritans or Workers or Independents, and so we can hardly be expected to possess a regal feeling for ballet. I'm not talking about the technique or the movement; I'm talking about the tradition, the style, the grand *royal* style in the classics.'

At the beginning of this chapter, Kenneth MacMillan remarked that, as a classical choreographer, he doesn't have the right feeling for modern dance; and modern-dance choreographer Paul Taylor has just said that he doesn't have the right feeling for classical ballet. What divides the two styles, then, is much more than different techniques – it is different attitudes.

A difference of opinion.

A *feeling*.

Chapter 3

PIONEERS AND FOUNDERS

Over the years modern dance has moved forward, upwards, downwards, sideways. Just about the only thing it hasn't done is remain the same. Unlike the different steps in classical ballet, which remain the same no matter in what order they are arranged, the numerous steps and gestures performed in modern dance will be as unique as the choreographer creating them.

Choreographer *A* will require her dancers to perform her work in one style. Choreographer *B* will demand another style. Choreographer *C* will create steps in his particular style. And so on.

Modern dance is obviously very different from classical ballet. But it is precisely *because* classical ballet existed that modern dance was born in the early years of the twentieth century. Certain pioneers were so bored by what they regarded as ballet's rigid formality and old-fashioned traditions, that they felt the time had come to do something about it.

So they rebelled.

The sort of dancing they wanted to break away from was largely the sort of dancing performed today by the Royal Ballet in London, the Royal Danish Ballet in Copenhagen or the Bolshoi Ballet in Moscow – that is, an entertainment taking the form of precise classical dancing and formal mime, performed to 'old-fashioned' music by Tchaikovsky, usually set against magnificent costumes and scenery, and meant to convey an idea or tell a story to the audience.

Dance of the absurd?

Swan Lake was exactly the sort of thing the dance rebels hated. A tale about lovesick maidens who are turned into swans, and who dance on the tips of their toes in the moonlight . . . this, they said, was absurd. It didn't reflect real life.

Looked at in this light, perhaps they were right. But then you could say that pop singers are also absurd to *sing* to us about love. That doesn't reflect real life either, because most people only *talk* about love. If you had to go up to your sweetheart and explain in song just how much you love him (or her), I'm sure you would get a very 'funny' look!

Anyway, what the dance rebels were furious about was a style of theatrical dance that can be traced back to France's dance-loving Louis XIV. In 1661, the king opened an academy of dancing. It was the first attempt to classify and record all that had been learned from the early masques of England and the Court banquets of Italy and France.

From that year to the present day we can trace a

direct line of ballet masters, dancers, choreographers and teachers. And from that year on dancing became regarded as an art in its own right, worthy of serious academic status.

Jumping steps and toe-dancing

In the eighteenth century a French musician's daughter named Marie Camargo caused a great sensation when she shortened her long skirt to just above the ankles. Yet modifying her costume in this way enabled her to introduce jumping steps. She also immortalised such beating steps as the *entrechat quatre*.

At this time, too, France's renowned dancing-master Jean Noverre had much influence on the movement towards greater freedom and his reforms led to a simplicity that greatly benefited the dance. In old prints, the great Italian-Swedish dancer Marie Taglioni is usually depicted wearing a style of costume that is still seen today – wreathed hair, low-necked, short-sleeved bodice, light, full skirts, and slippers.

Taglioni's appearance in *La Sylphide* in 1832 heralded the Romantic ballet movement, which reached its perfection in 1841 with Carlotta Grisi's portrayal of the heroine in *Giselle*. Most important of all, though, dancing on the tips of the toes (*les pointes*), appropriate to the fairy-like heroines of these ballets, came to be an essential step for women dancers.

Classical ballet reached its peak during the nineteenth century, notably in France with *Coppélia*, in Denmark with *Napoli* and a revised *La Sylphide*, and in Russia with *Swan Lake* and *The Sleeping Beauty*. It was a period of great choreographers like

Arthur Saint-Léon, August Bournonville and Marius Petipa, and fine ballet composers like Delibes and Tchaikovsky.

Revolt in Russia and America

The first important revolt against classical ballet occurred between 1909 and 1929 when a group of Russians, led by a talented theatrical producer named Serge Diaghilev, conquered Britain, France and other Western countries with exotic new works like *The Rite of Spring*, *Petrouchka*, *Schéhérazade* and *The Firebird*. Led by the choreographers Fokine, Balanchine and Massine, the designers Benois, Bakst and Picasso, the composer Stravinsky, and the dancers Pavlova, Karsavina and Nijinsky, and many others, ballet momentarily regained its artistic sincerity and seriousness.

The ballets of George Balanchine in America and Frederick Ashton in Britain have scaled new heights in beauty of form. But, since the death of Diaghilev in 1929, a genius has not yet emerged to advance the basic language of classical ballet and make it reflect the times in which we live.

And it is precisely for this reason that the modern dance movement came into being.

In a way, it had already started in America and elsewhere, when Isadora Duncan rejected ballet in favour of a style of dance that was strongly influenced by the art of ancient Greece. How odd that an ancient culture should form the basis of a modern artform!

Isadora Duncan changed the entire course of dance and inspired men like Fokine to a new awareness of the expressiveness of physical movement. She lived in a state of perpetual discovery: listening, looking, reading with a wonderful sense of the 'usefulness' of even the most trivial things that is granted only to artists of genius.

She was big in every sense of the word. She was not only big in personality and ambition but big in herself. When she died she weighed 81 kg. The story of her extravagant life and wild love affairs is told in a feature film starring Vanessa Redgrave and (as we saw in Chapter 2) in a full-length ballet by Kenneth MacMillan for Covent Garden, both called *Isadora*.

She was never beautiful, yet when she danced – bare-legged, bare-footed, in a see-through gauze shift – she shocked the capital of ballet, St Petersburg (now Leningrad), in 1904.

'It is as though you yourself were bathing in the music,' wrote an enraptured ballet critic.

Great men of the Russian theatre, such as Diaghilev, Fokine and Stanislavsky, agreed that from that moment the art of dance was changed for ever.

Starting-point of modern dance

At a time when people still marvelled at the new excitement of the moving pictures, and came under the spell of a liberating sound known as jazz, the impact Duncan made throughout the world with her dancing was little short of miraculous. Now, several decades later, the 'free', unsophisticated movements through which she used to express herself may strike you as being childlike – perhaps even laughable.

Yet they form the starting-point of modern dance as we know it today.

An extravagant life

Isadora Duncan (to the dance world she was known simply as 'Isadora') was born into poverty, in San Francisco in 1878, and, at an early age, found the inspiration for her particular form of dancing in Greek sculpture and architecture and in the rhythms of the waves. All the great events in her life, she claimed, took place by the sea.

Her greatest ambition – which she achieved through the generosity of a millionaire admirer – was to teach dancing to as many children as possible. She wanted to free their bodies from the prison of nineteenth-century narrow-mindedness in which she felt they were being held captive.

One woman who saw her perform was the American dancer Ruth St Denis, who was herself to influence a generation, including Martha Graham.

'At Isadora's performance,' recalls Ruth St Denis, 'there was no scenery, only simple curtains. Lighting was also simple. At first glance, Isadora herself may have seemed ordinary. She wore none of the fancy costumes of the period. She wore only a simple dress which looked rumpled and almost pinned up.

'Yet she walked on stage with such dignity and presence that all of us that were there that day were arrested. Then she began to move in tune to the cosmic rhythm of the Universe. I know those words must sound grand, but I can use no others.

'From then on, Isadora was The Dance.'

Frederick Ashton, British ballet's greatest choreographer, also calls to mind the first time he saw her dance. It was in 1921.

'Dressed in a Greek-style chiffon tunic,' reflects Ashton, 'she danced Brahms waltzes, Isolde's death and Chopin's Funeral March. With melancholy grace and irresistible intensity she moved through her new dance form.

'I was quite carried away and went back to see her time and time again. The way she used her hands and her arms, the way she ran across the stage – these I have adopted in my own ballets.'

Isadora was an inspiration to a great many people, not only to dancers like Ashton but to poets, painters, sculptors and musicians. Most of her life she wore a simple Greek tunic and sandals, for she felt that all the tight-laced corsets and underwear popular at that time was confining to the body's natural movements. She always wanted to set the whole world dancing, but it was her exploits rather than her dancing that made the news and headline stories.

She always did things in style. Gordon Selfridge, founder of the famous London department store that bears his name, sent her cases of champagne and (more practically) hampers of food, which followed her everywhere from the Sahara to the Russian steppes.

She died in France in 1927 in a manner which echoed the pattern of her life. While out with a handsome man in his open Bugatti sports car, driving along the Promenade des Anglais in Nice, her scarf became entangled in the spokes of one of the wheels, and she was instantly strangled. Ironically, like many of the significant incidents in her life, the accident took place by the sea.

She was a pioneer. She dreamed a beautiful dream and made it come true. She lived her life freely and fully: her ideals and talent were forty years ahead of her time. And yet, although she inspired people to better things and had the power to change lives, she passed on no lasting *style* – unlike Martha Graham.

Martha Graham's need to dance

Graham was born in 1894 into a middle-class Pennsylvanian household. Her father was a doctor interested in mental disorders. The family later moved to Los Angeles, where Graham attended a dance concert featuring Ruth St Denis, whose dancing was influencing people at the same time as Duncan's was.

'I knew after that performance,' she says, 'that I had to be a dancer.'

After attending the Denishawn School of Dance, run by Ruth St Denis and her partner-husband Ted Shawn, she finally became a major star of the Denishawn company. Later, during a two-year period with New York's Greenwich Village Follies, Graham grew restless with the routine of the job and began to feel a need to experiment with a type of movement that would 'plumb the depths of human emotion'.

As classical ballet seemed too artificial for her ('I didn't want to dance a flower'), she spent hours in front of the mirror discovering how the human body expresses passion, pain, joy, sorrow. A new dance form was slowly taking shape.

Unlike ballet, which tries to conceal the effort involved in carrying out a step, Graham *showed* the effort involved, spending as much time writhing on the floor as leaping in the air. As with Duncan, her costumes were very simple, her feet bare. Movements were often angular. Sudden – sometimes violent – thrusts of the torso, arms and legs replaced the flowing grace of classical ballet.

Thus the unmistakable technique of Martha Graham, and of modern dance as we generally recognise it today, was born.

But it was not until Graham was thirty-six that she enjoyed her first theatrical triumph. Her particular style of movement transformed ritual Indian dances into a celebration of life's mysteries.

Critics, for the first time, took note. People began to call her a genius. And that is what she is.

'The magic of gesture'

Martha Graham contributed more works to the theatre than any other woman in history: more than a hundred and fifty dance-dramas. For years she struggled and sacrificed, even endured ridicule, but her modern-dance technique is now to be seen throughout the Western world.

Actors such as Joanne Woodward, Gregory Peck, Henry Fonda and Lorne Greene have been to Graham to learn what she calls 'the magic of gesture, the meaning of movement'. Comic film actor Woody Allen was also a student. Modern dancers like Merce Cunningham, Anna Sokolow, Paul Taylor and Robert Cohan started with Graham. Even ballet's most famous superstar, Rudolf Nureyev, has been personally taught by her – and performed with her company.

The themes of her dances often look to the past for their inspiration. The magnificent legends of the ancient Greeks are a popular stimulus. Her style, however, has never looked anything but authentic and wildly original. One of her magical qualities is her ability to invent wonderful poses. Her technique *lives*.

Merce Cunningham's brand of anarchy

Merce Cunningham is one of the most important of all the many gifted choreographers to have emerged from the Graham company. In his dances, the factor of *chance* is very important. You will find little logical order in his works.

At the beginning of this century, as we have already seen, the great Russian producer Diaghilev established a formula for ballet where choreographer, composer, painter and dancer work in close consultation. Many years later, Cunningham went back to this basic formula, where the major creators cooperate equally in the production of a new work.

But the formula in Cunningham's case amounts to what he himself has called 'a kind of anarchy, where people may work freely together'. It certainly seems to work.

Steve Paxton, a leading American dance experimentalist and a former member of the Cunningham company in New York, recalls its impact on him: 'Perhaps only in the theatre can you fall in love with an entire group of people at once, and I fell in love with every one of Merce's dancers. But, above all, there was Merce himself. He is a movement genius, the intellectual becoming flesh, a *provocateur* with total discipline.'

'New Dance'

Anna Sokolow, Paul Sanasardo, Alvin Ailey, Dan Wagoner, Paul Taylor, Glen Tetley, Molissa Fenley, Karole Armitage, Charles Moulton, David Gordon and Alwin Nikolais are just a few of the many stimulating modern dance-makers to surface and blossom in the United States.

And now Britain can also boast modern-dance talent like Richard Alston, Siobhan Davies, Fergus Early, Janet Smith, Christopher Bruce, Ian Spink, Anthony van Laast, and the American but British-based Tom Jobe and Robert North. (The work of most of these dance-makers is described throughout the book, as well as in the Who's Who section of Chapter 14.)

The experimental area of dance, the *avant-garde* or ultra-modern, has in recent years been given a special name.

It is called 'New Dance'.

It has been described as a compromise between *formality* (that is, classical ballet) and *freedom* (modern dance). It flies as soon as it's over, remaining only vaguely in the eye. It is but a memory of those who danced and of those who watched.

Improvisation

Improvisation is an important part of this wing of experimental dance, pioneered in America by Yvonne Rainer. It produces semi-acrobatic, semi-military exercises and group names . . . choreography meant to be done by *anybody*.

Some of the other important names in American

New Dance are Trisha Brown (who starts with a movement problem – usually rather a simple one – and works until the group of dancers get good at it), Douglas Dunn, Kei Takei, William Dunas (he does very little, and what he does he does for a long time), Meredith Monk, Robert Wilson and Laura Dean.

But in Britain dancers have tended to flirt with this type of dance improvisation rather than take it seriously. Rosemary Butcher, Tamara McLorg, Mary Fulkerson, Fergus Early, Janet Smith, Maedée Duprés and Jacky Lansley have all tried their hand at it, none of them successfully.

Many of the dancers and choreographers mentioned here, and numerous others, will be reappearing in the following pages. Modern dance, as we shall see, certainly doesn't stand still.

Chapter 4

THE DANCER

Once, tired at being asked repeatedly why he dances
barefoot (it gives him better contact with the ground),
the American modern dancer and choreographer
Paul Taylor replied: 'So that my socks won't get dirty
and to save the laundry bills.'

Taylor's spoken humour, as in his ballets, is never
far away. But his reply hides the real reason as to why
modern dancers prefer to take their shoes off when
they perform. Like many other 'mysteries' in dance,
the answer stems from a very simple fact.

In very old societies the ground was looked upon as
a source of stability and strength, and so modern
dancers removed their shoes and performed with bare
feet in order to come in closer contact with the floor. It
strengthened their harmony and closeness with the
energy to be derived from the ground.

As an American critic noted: 'They could leap away
from it, but they also could bend and prostrate their
bodies on the floor to develop dance movement need-
ing such an impetus.'

Care of the feet

Another question the modern dancer is frequently asked is this: 'Isn't it hazardous dancing in bare feet? Doesn't it ruin your feet for life?'

Well, it *could*. Even the well-exercised feet of modern dancers are open to improper use. One secret is that dancers wash their feet a lot.

Their chief concern is the opposite of most people's. They want to *keep* the hard skin on their feet, not get rid of it. This means toughening them up with surgical spirit or meths.

Most dancers will tell you that their basic aim is to keep feet dry and cool, always to cut toenails straight across, and to relax off-duty in Dr Scholl's exercise sandals. Another dancer's tip is to always travel with a packet of Epsom salts for bathing feet at the end of the day.

By doing all this they usually manage to avoid trouble. And when you consider that modern dancers' feet must be among the hardest-working feet in the world, their advice is obviously worth following – even for non-performers with 'problem' feet.

Language of the hands

From feet to hands – and to the modern dancer, remember, the hand is many things. As it moves from the body it gives the audience an idea of direction. It may recreate an image. It may create a gesture of tradition, such as a clenched fist. Or it may simply help the dancer to achieve a better balance.

In modern dance, even more so than in classical ballet, there is no dance without the language of the

42

hands. They animate the body and call attention to its movements.

Martha Graham has often explained that her wonderful technique evolved from the cultures of Spain and the Orient. And you only have to look at the hand movements in her style of dance to see how true this is.

In Balinese dance, for instance, the hands are the flowers of the dance: they embellish all movement. In Chinese dance, each character type has its own posture and movement pattern. Even in the Flamenco dance of Spain, where so much attention is given to heel work, the hands and fingers become helplessly alive in the frenzy of the dance's colourful finale.

Discipline and muscular depth

The modern dance technique is a kaleidoscope of constantly changing steps, gestures and ideas. But wherever modern dance is performed, the style invented by Martha Graham is the yardstick or standard by which most dance-makers assess their own technique.

Pearl Lang, for many years a star of Martha Graham's company in New York, says: 'I teach the Graham technique because it prepares the body for a dynamic eloquence that can satisfy many different choreographic demands. After a real involvement in that discipline, a dancer's movement takes on a muscular depth, resonance and vibrato that no other technique seems to produce.'

The unique qualities of the Graham technique are dealt with in more detail in Chapters 5 and 7.

The modern dancer's 'easy' life

There is still a belief among many people that the modern dancer's life is so much 'easier' than that of the ballet dancer because the former doesn't have to worry too much about technique – that, in a performance, it is the artist's sincerity that counts, not how capable she or he is at doing fancy tricks.

Nothing could be further from the truth. The modern dancer works on her technique as tirelessly and devotedly as her colleague in the ballet company. She is never happy with her achievements.

The body as an instrument

Look at Judith Jamison. For many years she was one of the brightest jewels in Alvin Ailey's modern dance company in New York. Today she works as a guest artist in companies everywhere, and even occasionally takes a featured part in musicals.

Nobody has brought more lustre to the profession of modern dance than she has; and yet she will be the first to tell you, 'I still feel frustrated with my technique for much of the time, because it's hard to get things right, to get a dance to come out the way it is inside you, so that people can see it in your mind's eye.' Despite her tough self-criticism, however, she has won many awards. She was voted Dance Personality of the Year, for instance, by America's *Dance Magazine*.

She continues: 'I have to use my body like an instrument, and yet I always have to preserve it as *my being*. I obey the choreographer, but I am more than a choreographic instrument – because I am the kind of dancer who has to feel the dance in the pit of the stomach, in my head, as well as in my feet.'

But, most important of all, is her final remark: 'I am never satisfied unless the dance comes out right. It rarely does.'

So success for Judith Jamison has been brought about by self-will, hard work, determination and a personal ability to believe that, at any point in her daily dancing life, she should still be able to do better. It would be unthinkable for Miss Jamison to say to herself, 'Ah, at last – perfection!'

Perfection, for a dancer, is impossible to achieve. Perfection, too, is for tomorrow . . . and tomorrow never comes.

Ritual magic

'To perform modern dance is a way of life,' reveals Noemi Lapzeson, one of the founders of the London Contemporary Dance Theatre. 'Very few people understand the amount of hard work and pure physical demands it imposes on you to make your body reflective of emotions through movement, free to soar or remain motionless.'

Robert Cohan, artistic director (until 1983) of the modern dance company which he and Miss Lapzeson helped to start, then points out: 'Dance is ritual magic. That's why all the religions until now have included dance and magic as part of their ceremonies. It forces people to respond.'

'To perform modern dance is to be super-alive,' adds Paul Taylor. 'What modern dancers bring to the audience is not natural life, not real life; you can't, that's too good, you can't even expect to do that – but you *can* bring something that's a little bigger, a little more exaggerated.'

'Show off' steps frowned upon

One of the biggest differences between classical ballet and modern dance is that the first delights in showing its audience very difficult 'show off' steps whereas the second dislikes doing so. Virtuosity for the sake of virtuosity is frowned upon.

William Louther, a New Yorker now living in London, is one of the foremost modern dancers of his generation. He has danced with the companies of Alvin Ailey and Martha Graham in the United States and with the London Contemporary Dance Theatre in Britain; and this is why he won't fall into the habit of trying to impress with clever footwork:

'I can do as many pirouettes as you like: but I will not lift my leg higher than hip level, I won't jump higher than anyone else, I will not do as many tricks as possible, because that takes away from the work I am involved in and becomes to me the terrible frivolity of hell. Rudolf [Nureyev] is a nice friend, but he's never taken seriously as someone who is trying to communicate anything – he's a slave to being a peculiar kind of acrobat.'

How the young student of modern dance avoids becoming such an acrobat will be examined next.

THE YOUNG MODERN DANCER AT WORK

Chapter 5

THE STUDENT

The American modern dancer and choreographer William Louther explained in the last chapter why he, and others like him, dislike the sort of technical tricks on which classical ballet is so reliant. Now he reveals how he became attracted to dance.

As a boy he was appearing in the plays put on by his school in New York. One year, while rehearsing for one particular play, he discovered that the school's dance department was arranging a concert. When he saw the performance – the first show he had ever seen devoted to dance – he was completely bowled over.

He says: 'I'd studied tap when I was a little boy but hated it; and I considered ballet, from what I saw of the occasional *Nutcracker* on TV, a bit cissy. But that school concert was a revelation, my first look at *modern* dance.

'I remember trying to explain to my mother that it was the kind of dance we'd be doing in the future. The students had been doing all the basic things like walking and jumping and running, and I suddenly felt that in a few hundred years there would be a different way of walking down the street with a particular carriage of the arms and a sway of the back and a new use of the legs. I thought this was fascinating.'

He was twelve years old.

'I decided instinctively,' he adds, 'that dance would be the ideal way to express myself.'

And so, like every other boy or girl who has just discovered dance, he set about finding teachers. He went on to become one of the world's great male dancers.

Importance of the good teacher

William Louther was soon to learn that behind a great dancer there is always an equally great teacher. It is a fact of life, sadly, that these same teachers spend most of their time in unknown obscurity. They know little of the glamorous stage life, never sharing the applause and awards of those dancers they make into stars. In fact, they should be equally honoured.

The true teacher is noble, generous and sympathetic, urged on by his or her students' interest and desire to learn. He is strong but kind, serious, with a special sense of humour. He doesn't know how to be content because he is constantly working towards his goal of perfection.

Precision, discipline . . . perfection

The good dance student also knows that her target must not be short of perfection. Judith Jamison, whom we met in the last chapter, says: 'Dance is a very *perfect* thing. You give yourself to it, yet you have to prove your power over it.'

When American choreographer Paul Taylor takes a class in modern dance, he usually begins by telling his students: 'Dancing classes have to be very specific. You have to work for precision and discipline. It's an exact, *perfect* form.'

To return for a moment to Miss Jamison, she had reached a height of 172.72cm at fourteen years of age. On her sixteenth birthday she had grown 5cm more. But today her imposing, lovely, long-legged dancing is greatly admired. She is glowing proof that a female dancer can be tall *and* make a name for herself.

'For the dance to have power,' she says, 'the dancer must learn how to control it from her student days. Dance is too important for me to take it for granted just because, as a student, I learned some steps. It is too important for me to believe that all I need to do is go out there in a costume and let it happen. *I* have to make it happen.'

She is the first to admit that she would not be where she is today without the services of a good dance teacher. Nobody is closer to the dancer than the teacher. But a word of warning. A teacher's name may be 'famous' because of a reputation made during his or her earlier years as a dancer – and this can sometimes result in disappointed students, because the art of teaching is quite different from the art of performing.

One may be a great dancer but a mediocre teacher, and the other way round. A renowned dancer who is also a renowned teacher is rare. That must never be forgotten.

Dance schools are now training to a higher level than ever before. Dancers have to know ballet, jazz, tap, modern dance, and often take voice and drama lessons. Some students are so keen that they train seven days a week.

But a professional dance training, whether for Indian dance, ballet, modern American dance, or any other technique, offers something more than the acquired ability for the pupil to move his or her fingers in amazing ways, to spin round and round on the balls of his or her feet, or to fall unexpectedly backwards onto the floor.

A student dancer can discover that freedom is never acquired suddenly. A new freedom – the ability, say, to raise her foot a further 15cm – is gained only after days and months of continuous application and work. If he or she seeks such a new freedom in haste the result will only be pulled muscles and torn ligaments.

With proper training he or she can discover that sheer physical exhaustion is not something to be feared, a bottomless pit into which the body must be swept, never to return, but rather as an experience which may refresh and tone up the body as much as a good rest. Professional dancers know all about this.

For many years in the United States students have been able to prepare for degree courses in both classic and modern dance. Until recently, however, the only degree course open to dance students in Britain has been a scheme run by the Laban Centre for Movement and Dance in conjunction with the Council for National Academic Awards, although this is not geared purely to modern dance.

But in September 1982 the first university honours

degree in contemporary dance in Britain was introduced by the London Contemporary Dance School in collaboration with Kent University, a place of learning with a well-earned reputation for introducing exciting new ways of doing things. The degree course, for BA (Hons) in Contemporary Dance, is full time for three years and provides suitably qualified young dancers with a thorough education in dance, enabling them to reach the highest professional standards.

It embraces practical and creative aspects of dance, plus study of music, theatre arts and such theoretical subjects as anatomy and aesthetics. All students have to take part in the practical dance sections, although the course is not confined to those who wish to be professional dancers.

Each year, too, and quite separate from the degree course, the London Contemporary Dance School runs a Summer School. This offers a number of two-week courses in contemporary dance, José Limón technique, and ballet. There is also a one-week course in jazz dance.

The courses are graded from 'Beginners' to 'Advanced' and are open to students of all abilities – from those with little or no previous experience to those with a great deal of dance training behind them. They provide an ideal opportunity for those wishing to develop their dance skills by taking a short, busy, energetic course during the summer holiday period.

There is also a Junior Summer School. It offers two courses designed especially for students aged between nine and sixteen. There is never a dull moment!

If you want to find out more about the Summer Schools and the degree course, then write to the LCDS at the address on page 139.

Spirals, swoops and deep-breathing

What is the appeal of modern dance that attracts so many new pupils to it each year? Apart from the not unimportant fact that it permits people to embark on a dancing career much later in life than is the case in classical ballet, there is the attraction of the inspiring technical wizardry that must be mastered.

For instance – the spiral, the swoops into the floor, the back-fall. Many people, too, will be attracted by modern dance's *cool* qualities: the promise of being associated with an Eastern influence, including the arm movements more associated with some Oriental dance styles, and the deep-breathing of yoga.

William Louther recalls that one of the most important things he learnt from working closely with Martha Graham in New York was the valuable use of deep-breathing. He says: 'The beginning of every Graham class starts with breathing exercises. We start breathing quietly, which in itself is the beginning of movement. We extend that breathing so that the movement gets bigger: the breathing then activates the limbs: the limbs then react to the breathing and extend themselves. So it goes on until one is completely and totally moving.'

Correct use of the body

Even more important than good breathing is a well-proportioned body. It is to a dance what a Stradivarius is to a violinist: the perfect instrument for the supreme accomplishment of his art. Movement is also made easier, technique simplified.

At the beginning of their training, many dancers

will probably not have the ideal body; but, with sympathetic coaching, they will eventually learn how to deal with theirs sensibly. A student of modern dance, for instance, should be aware of her limitations and learn how to adapt to technical demands without 'forcing' her body.

It often seems quite unfair to some people that those who have the best bodies often don't have to work as hard as other less physically gifted students. Yet the student with a nicely proportioned body may develop into a technically weak dancer, while the less physically gifted student will perhaps be forced to work twice as hard and, in the end, become the better dancer.

Dancers with long legs are very much in fashion these days. No wonder Judith Jamison is such a winner! For some modern-dance choreographers, long-legged dancers are more than the favourite, they are the absolute.

How to achieve success

To sum up, then, two important factors are needed in order to achieve artistic success –
  1. Determination; and
  2. Perseverance.
Talent alone is not enough.

Why they studied the dance

We have seen how, as a boy, William Louther was drawn to modern dance. Now let us examine how a few other now-famous artists were attracted to modern dance.

Britain's foremost modern dancer and choreographer Christopher Bruce, for many years associated with the Ballet Rambert, confesses: 'Most working-class fathers wouldn't want a son of theirs to become a ballet dancer, but mine did. We'd just moved to Scarborough and he'd had a few drinks with the chap next door, who was a harmonica player, and this chap said he had a friend who ran a dancing school.

"Och," said my father in his broad Scottish accent, "Och, that'd be a marvellous career for my children."

And he got us out of bed at goodness knows what time in the early hours of the morning and said, "How'd you all like to be dancers?"

'Well, all the children went. I went, my brother went, and my two sisters went. My brother didn't stay very long; my sisters stayed on longer, but gradually they stopped dancing. I was the lone survivor.

'My father and the next-door neighbour started it all off . . . but for that fateful evening I wouldn't be doing what I'm doing now.'

'Can I do this, too?'

Anna Sokolow, American-born creator of modern dances such as *Dreams*, *Rooms* and *Deserts*, says: 'Dance was the first thing I ever saw that was beautiful. I was about eight years old and I saw a dance class in a settlement house for children. I think it was the barefoot style, the Isadora Duncan thing, tunics and all that.

'I walked in and said, "Can I do this, too?" And the teacher said "Yes." So I did, and that was the beginning.'

Like many modern dancers, America's Paul Taylor

began his training late, at twenty. It was the physical aspect of dance that attracted him, the simple fact that a dancer 'speaks' through his body.

Lar Lubovitch, another American dancer and choreographer, originally trained as a painter at art college. It was only afterwards that he became interested in dancing.

Glen Tetley's Alto-Classicism

Glen Tetley, the American choreographer who is as happy working with a classical company as with a modern one, says he didn't know such a thing as dance existed until he was eighteen years old. He grew up in a small, strict, religion-bound community in Cleveland, Ohio, where drinking, card-playing and dancing were frowned upon.

'When I discovered dance, well, I was thunderstruck,' Tetley remembers. 'It was the most miraculous thing, the first thing that made sense to me. But I was twenty before I actually started to dance, because earlier I was studying medicine.'

He had to take classes with boys and girls who were twelve or thirteen – 'and they were doing everything fantastically'. But eventually, as a trained performer, he was to work with every major modern dancer in America.

Tetley, in common with many dancers today, chose deliberately to be taught in both classic and contemporary styles. He is consequently one of the few first-league choreographers now working to have achieved a successful fusion of two very different styles in his dances. His productions for the Ballet Rambert, London Festival Ballet and the Royal Ballet, and for many companies on the Continent, all share the same happy mixture of 'Ancient and Modern'.

This 'mongrel' style, which I have called Alto-Classicism, will almost certainly became more and more common in the years ahead. Dance students in the future, I have little doubt, will be compelled to acquire a working knowledge of several styles if they hope to work freely and confidently with tomorrow's dance-makers.

Classical and modern-dance training

Donald McKayle, who has danced with Martha Graham, Anna Sokolow and Merce Cunningham, emphasises that 'in the way dance is developing in America, England and elsewhere, it is becoming essential to have training in both classical and contemporary dance styles – but you have to specialise sooner or later'.

Norman Morrice, for many years joint artistic director of the modern-style Ballet Rambert and since 1977 director of the classical-based Royal Ballet, agrees wholeheartedly with McKayle. He says: 'I think training in the schools of modern dance and classical ballet is healthy, but it should start early. At a given moment a dancer will choose between them: a choice often guided simply by physical shape; the demands of the classical technique ban certain people from performing that style. America has shown that it *is* possible to learn both styles.'

American modern dancer and choreographer Lar Lubovitch certainly insists that all dancers should be encouraged to train in both styles. 'But ultimately,' he adds, 'they should do the kind of dancing which feels most natural and beautiful for them to do. If it means training only one way, then that should be their calling.'

'It would do all classical dancers a world of good if they also combined classes in modern dance,' says the Dutch choreographer Hans van Manen. 'They would be concerned with a new feeling for the use of the body, and the moment they have tasted it I am sure they would also do things with it, because it is always a wonderful feeling to know that there are other ways available in which to express yourself.'

Using muscles in a different way

The ballerina Lynn Seymour discovered this 'wonderful feeling' a few years ago while she was choreographing her ballet *Gladly Sadly Badly Madly* for the London Contemporary Dance Theatre. She was then still a member of the Royal Ballet, but she thought it might be beneficial to embark on a course of contemporary classes.

'I'd never done a contemporary class before,' she explains, 'but I quickly found it very stimulating. I was using my muscles in a different way, and I'm sure that one type of dancing eventually helped the other.'

A word of warning, however, is offered by Maina Gielgud, a dancer familiar with many different dance styles. She says: 'I think it is important nowadays for so-called classical dancers to learn to use modern techniques, since they will have to employ them more and more with contemporary choreographers. But I am not sure that one should learn modern techniques before having a thorough knowledge of classical.'

Body alignment and balance

The American teacher Benjamin Harkarvy, who founded the Nederlands Dans Theater, is even more precise in his views concerning mixing classical and contemporary styles. 'I believe in classical ballet as the basic technique, to be studied daily,' he says. 'Well taught, it offers a scientific method developed over the past three hundred years. To this, other technqiues can be added – but only when the placement* and the use of the *plié*† are well set in the dancer.

'I consider these two components to be the physical foundation of a dancer's career. Anyone who wants to have a long career in dance must have both. A correct body alignment gives him the ability to control his balance, and a well-controlled *plié* is essential for the suppleness of his movement.'

Cross-fertilisation

The Martha Graham school in New York has such a respect for classical ballet, in fact, that it is now included in the curriculum – something which would have been unthinkable not so many years ago. In London, too, the Royal Ballet School now gives classes in contemporary dance. And most of the modern/jazz/rock dancers you see in television routines have enjoyed a basic classical ballet training – plus, of course, a wide experience beyond that.

---

* The holding of a dancer's body, head, arms and legs in their proper alignment to each other.
† Knee-bending exercise to make the joints and muscles soft and pliable, the tendons flexible and elastic, and to develop a sense of balance.

Cross-fertilisation in dance is not just a thing of the future. It is happening *now*. And it is something to which every student of dance must give his or her serious consideration.

Chapter 6

DANCE IN SCHOOLS – AND AS A HOBBY

Kate Flatt and her husband Tim Lamford, both modern dancers and choreographers, are among a small group of people who know what potential there is in the untapped dance talent in children all over Britain. Although Kate and Tim follow their individual careers as performers and dance-makers they also spend a great deal of time working in schools and colleges.

'There is a lot of exciting, raw talent which begins to show when children are given the opportunity to dance,' explains Kate, a Royal Ballet-trained teacher who devotes most of her time to modern dance projects. 'The British are freeing up a lot – partly, I think, because of the stimulus of the disco scene.'

Leeds is one of the provincial centres where, thanks to the effort and courage of local headmasters and teachers, dance has been given an important role in education. The effect of this has been speeded up by Arts Council schemes which have taken Tim Lamford to Leeds and had Kate Flatt based in an inner-city school. It is certainly much more than coincidence that as many as five students a year are being accepted by the London Contemporary Dance School from the Leeds area.

Physical strength

There are other schools in Yorkshire and Hampshire, to name but two counties, which have worked in dance for several years now and are consequently producing amazingly proficient youngsters who are going into the profession via schools like the LCDS. School children benefit in several ways from intensive classes. Kate explains that two groups she took in Leeds, in unselected classes of ten- and eleven-year-olds and more experienced twelve- and thirteen-year-olds, all gained physical co-ordination and strength from the daily ninety-minute classes.

'Getting physically stronger gives children more confidence in other areas of their work,' says Kate. 'I also insist that their writing and painting work should be linked to their dance experience to stimulate their imagination.'

When each course is coming to an end, Kate always choreographs a special modern-dance work for the pupils, perhaps using children's games or singing rhymes as the basis for it.

Modern dance at school

Many modern companies, in conjunction with the Arts Council – such as the Lancaster-based Ludus company – work with secondary school children. Some of the larger professional companies, like the London Contemporary Dance Theatre and the Ballet Rambert, also free their dancers for regular work with school children.

Children as choreographers

Since 1981, too, a novel company called Dance Experience for Children has been providing young children with a unique chance to watch and lend a hand in modern dance and music. The company is run by Maggie White, who is well-known for her teaching and choreographic work with young people, with the help of the musician and composer Alan Lisk.

The school programmes are split into two related parts. First, the children take part in a technique and choreographic class, where Maggie and Alan talk about the teamwork between musician and choreographer. The children then create their own dances, and are given help in composing their own musical accompaniment.

After the children have performed and discussed their dances, the company of five performers then present the second half of the programme, their own performance. The works danced are especially designed for young children and they show how the ideas previously discussed have been blended into the finished product.

In 1983, the company joined forces with the London Contemporary Dance Experience, of which Maggie White is the tour director. The company works in junior, middle and secondary school, colleges of further and higher education, arts centres and small-scale theatres, and the aim is to develop an understanding and enthusiasm about dance.

An alternative to P.E.

In broadminded schools all over Britain, dance is being included more than ever before in the curriculum – sometimes as an extension to the music class and often as an alternative to physical education. Wise teachers now realise that dancing, like soccer or netball, is good for you. It is healthy.

Modern dance as a hobby

It is also a lot of fun – as a growing number of young adults are discovering in everyday life. They, too, want to 'have a go'. So they are taking up modern dance as a spare-time hobby, in much the same way as others may take up photography or squash.

Some people may have studied classical ballet when they were younger, but have long since given it up. Others may never have received any dance training.

Modern dance appeals to both types of people because it can be 'picked up' gradually by the amateur without placing too great a strain on a body that is either untrained or 'rusty' through lack of regular exercise.

The classes themselves can be very stimulating, leaving the student with the same sort of physical well-being that a sportsman, say, feels after a round of tennis. All that is usually required is a leotard and tights, and a qualified teacher.

Tuition for modern dance, as well as for jazz and tap, is readily available all over the country at community halls, sports centres and evening institutes – plus, of course, at dance schools and commercial studios where part-time adult students are accepted. Dance is a booming business today. Everybody, from the professional to the amateur at the local discothèque, is doing it.

Chapter 7

FIRST COMPANY

For a young dancer straight out of school, the problem of securing her or his first job in a company will almost certainly prove to be the biggest hurdle she or he has yet had to face. It is a sad fact of life that modern dance, like classical ballet, trains far more aspiring dancers than there are companies available to accept them.

There will be many auditions and many disappointments. The graduate dancer, after perhaps ten or more years of study, must not be surprised to find herself suddenly 'unwanted' during the next twelve months or so. The fact that she cannot find a job may have nothing at all to do with any lack of talent or personality: it may mean simply that all the available companies are full up and cannot take on any additional dancers for the time being.

So, for the unlucky dancers, it will mean waiting until a vacancy exists and then applying yet again for a further audition. It will mean: keeping in constant touch with the modern dance companies, keeping an eye out for advertisements in periodicals like *Dance and Dancers*, *Dancing Times* and *The Stage*, keeping in touch with other dancers 'in the know' (what is called 'the grapevine') and, above all, keeping alive by taking a spare-time job until the lucky opportunity presents itself.

At the end of the book there is a list of modern dance companies, together with addresses and telephone numbers. The most important thing to be said about British modern dance groups like Mantis Dance Company, Midlands Dance Company, Extemporary Dance Theatre, Nin Dance Company, the Ballet Rambert and the London Contemporary Dance Theatre is that they are all essentially concerned with touring the country (but giving occasional London seasons).

To tour with a company that spends a great part of the year 'on the road', giving performances that range from weekly seasons to one-night stands, is to know what hard work is all about. Private life and socialising hardly exist, if they exist at all.

A dancer in such a company has to have a very understanding family. Most good dancers have 'caretaker' husbands or wives, 'caretaker' boyfriends or girlfriends, or 'caretaker' parents. There's no such thing as time off.

Stage-craft

The big bonus for the modern dancer, however, is that she will be called upon to dance much more frequently than soloists in a classical ballet company. It means she will learn about stage-craft and about her own capabilities much faster and more thoroughly than if she was given only one or two stage performances a week.

American modern dance choreographer Raymond Johnson, whose Raymond Johnson Dance Company is based in Woodstock, New York, says: 'Touring is the only way to learn about performing. You dance in big and small theatres before all kinds of audiences. And you have to be flexible because you don't always get the right equipment or space to dance in.'

A life on tour

Speak to a British dancer and his experiences will probably be little different to his American colleagues. Let's look, then, at the experiences of some dancers who tour with the London Contemporary Dance Theatre, which, though its headquarters are in London, devotes a great deal of the working year to touring.

If the company is visiting a theatre which is not too far from London – Oxford, say – the required scenery, costumes, and lighting and sound equipment will be loaded on to their lorry late the night before, the task being finished at perhaps 1.30 a.m. At 6.45 a.m., the stage crew will set off with their load for Oxford, arriving at the theatre at about 10.30.

Here, a relief crew of ten will begin unloading eleven tonnes of dance equipment. It takes about five hours to focus all the dance lamps – about one hundred and sixty of them – and another two hours to set up and test the sound equipment. It will probably be 9 p.m. before they are finished.

On top of this there is also the company's own floor surface to lay. This is usually made of a rubber-and-canvas material and helps to guard the dancers' bare feet against splinters.

At about 3 p.m. the next day the dancers can come on stage to do a class or rehearse.

The daily class

Tom Jobe, a tall American who only started to dance at the age of eighteen, says: 'We rehearse for two to three hours a day on tour, with a class lasting one and a half hours. When you get up in the morning, feeling all tight and sore, you sometimes think you don't want any more . . . but after fifteen minutes of class you feel better.'

A Graham class usually starts with all the dancers seated on the floor, in readiness for the floor work that is such an important feature of the Martha Graham technique used by this and other modern dance companies. And it is extremely difficult.

Preparing the torso to be flexible

Perhaps you are asking, 'Why use the floor?' Well, as Graham herself has said, a class is a life in miniature, a period of gradual growth.

Imagine it in terms of the baby who cannot stand and so spends some time on the floor until it is strong enough to stand upright. The dancer, similarly, prepares his torso to be flexible and strong enough for proper carriage when he stands.

Remember: The spine is the tree of life.

The floor, as an element in choreography, is invaluble as well. In pieces such as Graham's *Night Journey*, based on the Oedipus story of ancient Greek

70

legend, staccato jumps and precise falls and recoveries give tremendous excitement and range.

Exercises for the legs, hips and feet, and for turning movements, come next in the daily class. This is followed by exercises for elevation (leaps, skips, runs, jumps and turns in the air). The use of fall and recovery (or contraction and release), involving the complete inhalation of breath (contraction) and of utter exhalation (release), conclude the class. It is all part of the modern dancer's tough working day.

Digs and landladies

'We have one month off a year,' adds Tom Jobe. 'But near the end of your vacation you're itching to get back. Dancing is an addiction: you get depressed without it.'

Celia Hutton, relaxing in a cold, stone-floored dressing-room, explains: 'Some weeks, touring is hell. In Canterbury once there were no showers at all and out of the cold water tap came nothing but yellow slime.'

She reflects: 'It's worse for the boys. They sweat more and they have to put on body make-up and they go back late at night to their digs and the landlady says, "Oh, no. Baths are only between 8 a.m. and 9 a.m." At the end of a tour we're always very tired. But you have to go on dancing.'

It is this curious *need* to dance which keeps the performers in one tolerably content and happily integrated unit throughout such gruelling tours . . . tours hampered by cheap, inadequate accommodation; by under-heated stages and furnace-like dressing-rooms; by the bulbless light fixtures by which they make up; by stages which are often so small that they do not have wing space or fly facilities to hold lighting equipment and no place for the dancers to stand while waiting in the wings for their entrance.

It is a challenge and a gamble which this enterprising company, and almost all the smaller modern companies, willingly tolerate just so that they can go on dancing: the very thing to which they are addicted like others may be addicted to potato crisps or Tom and Jerry cartoons.

Diet

A correct diet is only second in importance to warming-up in a dancer's day, and with so few hours in that day he tends to set up a pattern for food as automatically as he sets up for his stretches. A dancer's body is a sensitive, refined, well-composed machine, and only the right food can make that machine operate properly.

The great American dancer and choreographer Murry Louis has made a particular study of diet in a dancer's life. 'A dancer is very consistent with his loyalty,' he says. 'He will swear the same devotion to each new diet he undertakes.

'He'll offer himself as living proof that his current nutriments work – that is, until they don't work. Then he becomes an authority on their failure.'

What, how and when to eat

He goes on to say that since food becomes such a personal matter, and eating away on tour has become so impersonal, dancers, like hermit crabs, have taken to carrying a bit of their home with them – their kitchens – when they go on tour. A great many of the grains and non-additive foods that are popular in today's diet are not available or else difficult to find 'out there', and as a result dancers travel laden like pack-horses.

'There are two critical meals for a dancer,' explains Murry Louis. 'These are breakfast and the perform- ance meal. Breakfast is obviously the first meal after awakening and is not much of a problem.

'But the performance meal is tricky. Some dancers can eat a large meal before performing and need to do so, while others must eat after the show. For myself, five o'clock in the afternoon is the absolute latest I can put anything into my stomach, other than chocolate. I wouldn't get ill if I ate later, I would simply fall asleep.'

Disappointments – and success

It should be obvious by now that to succeed in modern dance, as in classical ballet, a young man or woman must be tough. We have already seen that early disappointments are not only likely but must be ex- pected.

Success in dance, though, is usually just ten per cent talent and ninety per cent *luck* – being in the right place at the right time. Yet success should not be the 'be all' and 'end all' in a young dancer's career.

There have been few more successful people in modern dance than America's Judith Jamison, who appeared for many years with Alvin Ailey's American Dance Theatre. 'It is nice to be successful, after you've worked so hard to achieve something,' she says. 'We all want to be admired. To be respected in your profession must be the greatest thing there is.

'But,' she is quick to add, 'success of any kind only forces you to work harder, because then you carry the responsibility for the success. I am responsible to myself, to the dancers I work with, to the choreographer whose work is set on me. Success can be tough.'

Chapter 8

CREATING A DANCE

Cliff Keuter's rehearsal studio on West Broadway, New York, is white, with a pale yellow floor. The dance area is clear, but scattered all around the fringes is accumulated stuff – props from or for past or future dances (a red wagon, a large pickle barrel, a rubber tyre, a sawhorse, an umbrella) – plus a television, two tape recorders, some loudspeakers, and lots of tapes and records.

Keuter is rehearsing *Wood*, a work in his modern dance company's repertory that is new to dancers Ellen and Bill De Young. Dance-maker Keuter gives instructions, using non-dance terms like 'squiggly':

'Billy, as you come out of it, the movement must become very calming. Press the air down in front of you.'

Then: 'No, it's not supposed to be sexy. It's about tought street kids.'

And: 'Don't lose the clarity, the *specificity* of the movement . . .'

As the rehearsal goes on, the dancers give each

other corrections. They stop and ask questions. Keuter, whose dances possess a touch of madness, answers them. The rehearsal then proceeds.

'I think I sometimes create dances in my dreams, and I like that,' says the choreographer from Idaho who once danced with the Paul Taylor company. 'I like to feel that I'm always prodding. Asking for more.'

'Bam, bam, bam, bam . . .'

When he is making a new dance, Cliff Keuter is a great task-maker. So is Alvin Ailey, the Texan choreographer whose works in recent years have achieved a sort of halfway point between modern dance and ballet.

When choreographing a new work, Ailey somehow stimulates movement into his dancers with a combination of verbal and body English. I remember watching him at work in his New York studio. He was creating his most famous ballet of all, *Revelations*, which explores in exotic and lively dance the accompanying score made up of Negro spirituals.

He switched on a tape recorder. 'Bam, bam, bam, bam, three, four, five, six, seven, eight,' he bellowed at dancer Freddy Romero, who moved swiftly to the counts.

Ailey got up from the floor and demonstrated the sort of movement he had in mind.

'What kind of turn was *that*?' asked Romero, as he attempted to copy it.

'Who knows?' answered Ailey.

He laughed.

Romero did the step again – and again and again.

Each time he went over that dance phrase he heightened the movement and enriched the line.

'You've got it!' Ailey called out. 'That's it!'

Six seconds of choreography had been created. The tape was rewound to the beginning and Romero started all over again, polishing those six seconds until the steps achieved near-perfection.

Bubble gum philosophy

Most modern dance choreographers create works at a much faster pace than choreographers working in ballet, and let their old works drop out of the repertory sometimes after only one season, because they feel variety really is the spice of life. By performing old works over and over again for many years, they argue – and I think they may be right – they leave little room in the performing schedule for creating and displaying new productions.

'You can keep on chewing bubble gum for ten hours,' says the gifted American modern dance choreographer Twyla Tharp, 'but after a minute-and-a-half you've gotten all the good out of it.' Why not replace the old bubble gum (that is, the old production) with a new piece? That's what Miss Tharp is saying.

Having new works created for them is what keeps dancers happier than anything else in the world. They like it. Critics like it. Most audiences like it. And, of course, choreographers like it.

The word choreography is a combination of two Greek words – *khoros*, meaning dancing, and *graphia*, which means writing. A choreographer, therefore, is somebody who writes (or composes or creates) a dance or a series of dances.

He is a sculptor of movement. He will use the dancer's body in much the same way as the sculptor works in clay: he will try a movement this way and that way, and if he is not satisfied with the result he will discard the idea and try again.

Let us suppose we are in a rehearsal studio, which may be a vast airy room with perhaps two or three mirrored walls, and the dancers who have already been chosen by the choreographer for the new dance are assembled there. The music has already been chosen or specially written, and will either be played on a piano or (if an existing recording is being used) relayed from a tape or long-playing record.

The choreographer will express a particular movement or step, perhaps pointing out how this figures in relation to the proposed new work as a whole. From this, often vague, instruction the dancer enlarges upon it and carries it out in a way she thinks the choreographer would like to see it performed.

She will probably interpret the phrase of movement the way *she* thinks best, while perhaps offering suggestions for improvements or further steps or a new approach entirely. And probably if the choreographer approves, the dancer's conception of the movement will be the one finally taken into the dance.

Working methods

How modern dance choreographers go about creating a new work varies as greatly as do their individual personalities. The following five choreographers tell us how *they* prepare new dances (the first two men are Dutch, the others American).

Hans van Manen: 'I never do a rough outline on paper for a new piece. Ideas come to me higgledy-piggledy. I put all my thoughts into a big hat and I take them out in the studio when I am creating.'

Rudi van Dantzig: 'I plan everything and know just what I want to do when I arrive at the studio. I can't take the risk of letting dancers wait about and then find myself uninspired. I always have to be prepared.'

Lar Lubovitch: 'Usually I've listened to the music many, many times before I get to the studio, and often I'll dance to it in my apartment – just letting myself improvise, fall around and do whatever feels right to me at the moment.

'I never know what the ideas are. I don't even think about them. I just let myself shift around to the music. It means that, although I haven't prepared anything, a lot of those things will feed back when I get to the studio.'

The starting-point

Glen Tetley: 'For me the most interesting way to start a new work is to prepare a kind of framework in advance, which is the score, and to go into the studio and begin absolutely cold with the dancers. So the starting-point then becomes movement, and from the movement one begins to bring in other things, such as recent experiences you have gone through.

'It takes on its own life, and for me this is the most exciting way to work, because you don't stop a flow of ideas or a flow of movement before it's had a chance to be discovered. Everything becomes possible: you don't restrict yourself to a certain area.

'I don't use any written "plot" or synopsis. I don't draw any little diagrams in advance. I already know a general idea I wish to go into, which can be both emotional and physical, so to me it's of no help to put it down on paper.'

Collaboration

Louis Falco: 'I use a number of different processes in making a dance. For instance, with my first work, *Argot*, I found the music; I had the dramatic idea and knew exactly what I wanted to do, then I created the movement to the music.

'In *The Gods' Descent* I had already started to create the characters and the movement when I began to look for the music, which was a collage of many composers. The same thing happened with *Huescape*.

'But when I started doing *Caviar* everything worked together as it went along. The music was being composed by a rock group, the sculptress Marisol was sculpting the fish which are such an essential part of the work, and I was creating the choreography. That was a complete collaboration and that's the way I prefer to work.'

It is also how, ideally, most major choreographers prefer to work: collaborating equally with the composer, designer and lighting director. If the choreographer is using music that is already commercially available on disc then, of course, he has one less collaborator to worry about.

The music

You have seen how some choreographers cannot begin work on a dance until they have found a suitable piece of music, or until the score specially written has been played to him. The English dancer and choreographer Janet Smith *always* starts with the music first.

She says: 'Phrasing and rhythmic patterns are the essence of dancing as they are of music. So music is important to me at a very early stage in the working out of a dance. It may even be the motivation: the dance images coming from the images the music evokes.'

But not all choreographers find it helpful to create steps *to* the sound of music. 'To me,' says Glen Tetley, 'the working basis would be destroyed if I did that.'

He adds: 'Before I start to work with a piece of music, I listen to it – *and then I put it away*. I don't want to have my ear destroyed by hearing it over and over again. Each time I hear that music, I want to hear it as if I've never heard it in my life before.'

Pop music and Jelly Roll Morton

Modern dance choreographers have always been interested in electronic music, and synthesised music, ever since it was invented. Jazz, too.

But it was not until the American choreographer Twyla Tharp came along that serious dance-makers utilised pop music on a large scale for their works. It may seem difficult to imagine this now, when every modern dance choreographer uses rock, soul, country, punk music, and even ballad singers such as Frank Sinatra and Engelbert Humperdinck, for their creations.

For her inspiration, Miss Tharp went to the Beach Boys and Chuck Berry, to Fats Waller and Jelly Roll Morton. She had also used classical masters like Bach, Mozart and Brahms (all very popular with other modern-style choreographers as well), but it was pop music in dance which she really made respectable to audiences.

Coming at a time when modern choreographers had been showing a great liking for the sound of rain, wind, broken glass and all manner of squeaks, gasps and scraping noises for their 'scores', the use of a familiar pop group was an absolute novelty.

Costumes and décor

After the dance steps and the music comes the décor – the designs for the costumes the dancers are going to wear and the designs for the props and scenery that will decorate the stage or performing area. Modern dance can exist, and does exist, without stage designs, plain drapes often being the sole adornment; and costumes are frequently plain leotards and practice tights.

But even modern dance, which tends to regard elaborate stage and costume designs as too close to classical ballet for comfort, can be considerably enriched by the services of a sensitive and inventive designer. Such a person is Nadine Baylis, one of the world's top dance designers. She has been associated for many years with the Ballet Rambert, where her stage sets, as well as her costumes, are known for the economy of their design.

'The important thing in modern dance,' she says, 'is to be able to see the body working. I've tended to specialise in very tight costumes, painted in such a way that you can see every muscle working.'

Miss Baylis begins work when the choreographer is about halfway through creating a piece. She spends part of each day attending rehearsals, where the initial search is to find a particular *image* for the dance. She says there is no greater thrill than to start work on a new modern dance.

Some other designers whose work you can expect to see in modern dance are Liz da Costa, Norberto Chiesa, Peter Farmer, Barney Wan, Andrew Storer, Antony McDonald, Judy Sterdman, David Buckland, Ralph Koltai, Robert Rauschenberg and Isamu Noguchi.

The lighting designer

In recent years the man or woman responsible for illuminating the stage has taken on an increased importance. One of the major lighting designers in British dance is John B. Read, who has built up a special relationship with the Ballet Rambert and the London Contemporary Dance Theatre. He usually starts work on a new production about ten days before the première, taking notes and plotting in his mind how he thinks the lighting should be utilised.

He explains: 'When I start the actual lighting I have a complete programme in my head of how I want it to look. But if I see a certain development, certain colours, certain angles of light working beautifully, I'll develop that and "play" within my framework. Although it's all planned beforehand, and although I work relatively quickly now, it is exhausting work.

'I get the dancers to "mark" the piece on stage in

slow motion, and I tend to light between six and ten cues to the hour. A modern ballet can have up to forty cues in a work lasting forty-five minutes, and after about fifteen or twenty cues I long to stop for ten minutes . . . but when I've got the dancers there I *can't* stop.'

The choreographer in another world

When a choreographer is creating a new work, his senses seem to take on a new life and he seems to be operating in another world. 'I'm completely preoccupied when I'm working on a new piece,' says Ian Spink, an Australian modern dance choreographer working in London. 'At such a time I find it difficult to do even day-to-day things like making phone-calls and doing the shopping.'

'Choreography,' adds Paul Taylor, 'is a very soul-consuming involvement and I must say I don't look forward to it each time. I think if I ever made a dance that was really good I'd stop choreography completely – but I've never made a dance that I'm totally proud of. Never.'

So, for the time being, Taylor is still making dances that are beautiful to look at, and very often humorous too. Most modern dance choreographers share his sort of self-doubt: it is such a self-doubt that, in time, turns a merely good dance-maker into a great one.

Curtain-up

And when the new dance work is completed, what then? Listen to Glen Tetley: 'The worst moment in the creation of a new ballet is when you finally finish it.

The process of creativity suddenly stops but the machinery wants to go on.

'When you're in the rehearsal studio it's your own world. But then you get to the point where you have to transfer it to a stage. Here you have to meet the problems with the stage staff and designers and so on.

'It's like letting a child go. You've got to say, "You're on your own now." You've got to let it live its own life and have its own identity. You can't "play" with it any more.'

And so the curtain goes up on another new dance.

Third Step

SHOW BUSINESS
DANCING
– AND THE FUTURE

Chapter 9

JAZZ DANCING – AND TAP

'What,' someone asked the American choreographer Alvin Ailey, 'is jazz dancing?' He replied that for him it was any dancing to jazz music.

Jazz baffles people who feel they must have neat definitions. Jazz music and jazz dance are essentially American artforms which can be traced back to Africa. They express the need for freedom that carried black people through slavery and subsequent discrimination.

Today, jazz dancing is vibrant and dazzling. It is so spectacularly irresistible that even a leading classical performer like Mikhail Baryshnikov jumped at the opportunity to dance a jazz duet with Judith Jamison, in Ailey's frisky *Pas de Duke*.

Jazz has taken on many appearances. It is Broadway show dance and movie musical dance. You see it in television shows, in glamorous nightclubs, casinos and discothèques. Hollywood stars Ginger Rogers, George Raft and Joan Crawford all began as jazz dancers.

Where did the word *jazz* come from? Legend has it that a soulful piano player was asked, 'Just what is that haunting music you're playing?'

'I'm just jazzin' around,' he answered. 'Just messing around. It doesn't have a name. It's just the way I feel right now.'

In other words, it has to do with improvisation. Making something up on the spur of the moment.

Difficult to teach

In jazz dance, no movement is dull. It is infectious, fancy, tricky, showing off the body with quirky, subtle moves. It is also very difficult to teach, because it is not a *specific* style of movement or thinking.

Despite this difficulty, however, jazz has become one of the most popular forms of dance for study, especially in the United States, by students of all ages. Teenagers, not surprsingly, love the music. They love the way that jazz takes in their latest dance fads. Young children, particularly, have a lot of fun.

Others find that jazz gives them the exercise they want and an emotional release from their daily routine. Some say that jazz dancing provides the same enjoyment and escape as going to the cinema to see favourite stars like John Travolta, David Essex or Toyah.

But learning jazz dance alone will limit the student. Ideally, it should be studied (at all levels) along with ballet, tap and modern dance. The outcome will almost certainly be a much better dancer.

Remember: Jazz dance is to classical ballet what jazz music is to classical music. Jazz dance improvises on basic, defined ballet movements.

A student of jazz is required to contribute a part of herself in order to become a dancer. She can learn the movement, the rhythm, even the teacher's 'feel', but then she must improvise within certain limits. This undoubtedly accounts for the popularity of jazz dance.

It is fun.

The only complete artform?

Eva von Gencsy, a former ballerina of the Royal Winnipeg Ballet and of Les Grands Ballets Canadiens, and later artistic director of Montreal's Les Ballets-Jazz, discovered that jazz dancing was, for her, the only complete art form. A great many dancers feel the same way.

'Jazz was a revelation to me,' she says. 'As a Hungarian I feel an intense need for self-expression. Although I love ballet, it did not allow me to completely express myself, as jazz does.'

The American dancer Ann Reinking was a veteran of such Broadway musicals as *Fiddler on the Roof*, *Cabaret*, *Pippin*, *Chorus Line* and Bob Fosse's *Dancin'* before she was thirty (she was born in 1951). In *Dancin'* she was involved almost entirely in jazz dancing. Yet a large part of her daily training is in the ballet style – 'because I think it's the best'.

Miss Reinking, who has worked with such top Broadway choreographers as Michael Bennett, Onna White and Michael Kidd, explains: 'You don't get enough strength from jazz, you don't get enough discipline, you don't get enough real warm-up. So I go to ballet, just because it's healthier for me. I find that if I get stronger in my ballet technique, then my jazz technique improves, too.'

The reverse is also true. Classical dancers such as Mikhail Baryshnikov and Rudolf Nureyev perform a lot better once they've learned other techniques, including modern and jazz. There is a wonderful looseness about jazz which really adds another dimension to a ballet dancer's training.

And on television, almost every night of the week – in shows such as *Top of the Pops* – you can see jazz dancers performing with tremendous vigour and ability. They have become an important part of our television-viewing lives. (See Chapter 11.)

Fame, an American film made in 1980 about teen-aged student dancers and singers at New York's High School for the Performing Arts, relied tremendously for its impact on the vibrancy of jazz dancing. The film was later made into a very successful television series and, even later, into a glamorous stage show called *The Kids from Fame*, which toured all over the world.

Jazz tap dancing

Inseparable from jazz dancing is jazz tap dancing. In recent years there has been a great revival of interest in this exuberant showbiz entertainment, thanks largely to the many concerts given by three of the world's leading masters of tap – the Americans Honi Coles, Chuck Green and Will Gaines. They have appeared many times in Britain (including at the annual Dance Umbrella festival) and on British television, while Chuck Green's jazz tap film *No Maps on My Taps* has won him many new young fans.

Tap dancing is itself a valuable exercise for the muscles of the legs and feet, made up of various combinations of taps, beats and steps. There are many movements and steps, described by such names as hop, spring, walk, brush, skuff, stomp, skuffle, flap, dig, pick-up, and wing. The tap dancer's hips, ankles and knees must be flexed, the arms relaxed, and the body moved in rhythm with the feet.

Dancing with Count Basie

Honi Coles' career spans more than half a century and has made him one of the finest exponents of jazz and tap dance today. He appeared on Broadway in *Hello Dolly* and in the hit musical *Bubbling Brown Sugar*, and in 1980 he staged the dance numbers for a new Broadway musical about one of the most famous black dancers in the world, Bill 'Bojangles' Robinson, who died in 1949.

He explains: 'You could say that tap dance is the only truly American dance, though maybe jazz and modern dancers make a similar claim. I think it's that combination of African syncopation and footwork from British folk dances like the jig and the clog that make jazz tap so special.'

Coles says that, like so many dancers of his generation – he was born in 1912 – he was 'hooked' on tap dance from a very early age. 'Tap was fun, it was entertainment, we all wanted to do it,' he tells people. 'I got kicked out of school because of my bad attendance record. So I used to get together with my friends and we'd have a tap dance jamboree.'

Honi Coles went on to appear in every major American variety theatre, from coast to coast, with such great names in jazz as Count Basie, Duke Ellington and Louis Armstrong. He was the creator of so-called 'centipede steps' – phrases that seem to go on forever and not repeat themselves.

An alternative dance entertainment

Young hoofers today regard Coles' partner, Chuck Green, as the godfather of jazz tap. He was born in Georgia and began dancing on pavements in Atlanta. He has been called both the 'Bach of tap' and the 'King Lear of tap'.

Will Gaines, the third man in the great tap trio, is one of the few remaining American jazz tap dancers from the vaudeville tradition, and has now made England his home base. In his time he has worked with most of the great names of jazz, rock and variety, from Duke Ellington, Billie Holiday, Lena Horne, Judy Garland and Lenny Bruce to Aretha Franklin, Charlie Watts and Ian Dury.

Today he tours a great deal in Britain with the Humphrey Lyttelton Band, Max Collie's Rhythm Aces, the Ed Speight Quartet, the Midnite Follies Orchestra, and other bands. He and other performers like him are living proof that outside ballet, modern dance, discothéques and musicals there is an alternative dance entertainment with a persuasive new fan following.

Chapter 10

DANCING IN CABARET AND THE COMMERCIAL THEATRE

Not all dancers, as we have seen, are suited to classical ballet. They may be the wrong shape. They may suffer from a physical weakness, such as a hip complaint. Or they may simply lack the right temperament. Whatever the reason, one thing is clear: if they wish to capitalise on their many years of study, they must use their talents in other areas of dance.

Just as Sarah Noble did.

'I began my training in the usual way, by studying classical ballet,' she says. 'But I soon realised that I'd never make it as a ballerina. I was too tall and my thighs were too big.'

So, instead of giving up, she decided to exploit these 'faults'. She now lives in Paris, where she dances at the spectacular Paradis du Latin nightclub. 'I found in the end the answer to all my dreams,' says Sarah today. 'I love dancing, and I'm doing a lot of it – in glamorous surroundings.'

British girls are best

Phyl Payne has been running an agency since 1953 which selects and looks after British dancers who work in such glamorous overseas nightspots. She only handles engagements that provide the Standard Overseas Contracts issued by the British actors' and dancers' union, Equity, and she prefers girls to be eighteen or over.

She explains that although talented dancers are not especially difficult to find, it is very hard to get people who are tall enough. Girls need to be between 167.64cm and 175.26cm, and when boys are required they must be at least 177.8cm tall.

Miss Doriss of the Moulin Rouge is her biggest client. They've worked together for years. Auditions for her Parisienne troupe, Les Doriss Girls, are held frequently in London.

But why London?

'Because,' says Miss Payne, 'British girls are still the best dancers in the world for this sort of work.'

When dancers are treated like cattle

The American choreographer Michael Bennett, son of a Sicilian engineer, once danced as a member of the chorus in dynamic shows like *West Side Story* and *Subways Are for Sleeping*. So many years later he devised the musical *A Chorus Line*, with a score by Marvin Hamlisch, as a tribute to his profession.

In two hours, without an interval, it shows how a

theatre producer lines up dancers like cattle and makes them work themselves to exhaustion, and open up their private lives, so that he can choose the best for an imaginary show. 'I wanted to show how it really is,' he said at the time.

I have 'sat in' on many auditions for musicals. It really *can* be soul-destroying.

It is the same for dancers who hope to appear in summer shows all over Britain, such as *The Jim Davidson Show* or *Seaside Special*. Most girls apply for these jobs by answering advertisements in *The Stage*, the theatre people's weekly newspaper. They will scan the pages for announcements like 'Wanted: Dancers'.

Into springtime London they flock. Girls straight from dancing school: some who have tried to get into a classical ballet company and failed, some who have wintered in pantomime and spent the out-of-work (or 'resting') months as shop assistants, barmaids or clerks. One or two may have been lucky enough to work in a rare touring musical.

They wait in their scores outside audition halls all over Britain, though mainly in London . . . a queue of pretty girls with little attache cases, bright smiles and new hairdos, awaiting their turn.

'What can you do?'

The piano stamps out.

In two minutes a girl's summer, her career, her life, can be decided. For were not Audrey Hepburn, Millicent Martin, Shirley MacLaine and Goldie Hawn discovered in dancing troupes too?

It is a thought for the queue. Another thought: some dancers try year after year, always fail, and always will fail. But a few, about one in every forty at a mass-audition, will get a contract.

How a dancer *looks* at auditions for summer shows, pantomimes and musicals can make all the difference between getting a job and losing it. The choreographer Rex Grey has been holding auditions for more than a quarter of a century for dancers hoping to secure work in the commercial theatre, nightclubs, casinos, hotels, restaurants and ocean-going liners, so he is a man well worth listening to.

He says: 'The trouble with auditions is that people don't bother to read advertisements properly in trade papers like *The Stage*. Even though I may specify stage make-up and rehearsal dress, girls turn up without make-up, their hair a mess, no tights or shoes, and expect to be considered for a job.

'Or I'll ask for girls who are five foot or over – and short girls will travel all the way down from the North of England hoping to make me change my mind. It's an appalling waste of money.'

Nerves and vulnerability

English choreographer Gillian Lynne manages to switch with impressive ease from West End musicals to grand opera, from straight theatre to television and films. In any given week she may be creating a dance routine for the Muppets, coaxing an ice skater into a ballet solo for a Royal Variety Performance, or choreographing a West End show such as *Cats*.

So she is always auditioning dancers for her shows, which embrace the whole glamorous world of entertainment; and she worries like mad in case she misses any real talent.

She says: 'It's a terrible thing, sitting in judgement, trying to allow for nerves, and trying to guard against the person who is marvellous at auditions but is never going to get any better.

'They come up to you afterwards. They know they've been good, but you just say "Thank you very much". You see a puzzled look in their eyes. They can't understand why they haven't got the job. But how do you explain that you're looking for *vulnerability* – you don't want that sureness, that theatrical brightness that curbs any sensitivity?'

When auditions were being held a few years ago for a West End production of *The King and I*, starring Yul Brynner and Virginia McKenna, I saw two hundred hopeful dancers going through their paces at the London Palladium in the morning, a further two hundred in the afternoon. Literally hundreds of unsuccessful dancers were rejected as 'unsuitable' that day.

The American-Japanese dancer-choreographer Yuriko, for many years a star of Martha Graham's company in New York, was restaging Jerome Robbins' original choreography for this production. She told me afterwards how dancers feel at auditions like these.

'When they get eliminated,' she explained, 'they'll be thinking, "Well, I'm just as good as that person. Why did they throw me out?" We just don't have the time to tell them. And they'll *never* know.'

Trying to impress the producer

Disappointed show dancers can take heart from the experience of Bob Fosse, the energetic American choreographer who first brought *Cabaret*, *Sweet*

99

Charity and *The Pajama Game* to the stage. Today he sits in on many auditions, choosing the sort of dancers he wants for his forthcoming musicals. But this former dancer has never forgotten the years when *he* had to try to impress producers with *his* dancing skills.

'When I went for auditions,' he says, 'I was sick for three days before. Literally sick. I'd just pray that the whole thing would be cancelled.

'You know, I never got a part from an audition – only from someone having seen something I'd done before. It's the only consistent thing about me.'

When he holds auditions, therefore, he is very conscious that the dancers trying to impress him are really going through the same mental agonies which he, as a dancer, suffered at such times.

Qualifications needed

What are the qualifications required to secure jobs in the commercial theatre? Joe Layton, the American choreographer who creates the dances for productions ranging from Broadway musicals to Royal Ballet pieces, explains: 'Dancers in musicals, at least the ones that I employ, must be brilliantly trained. I never use dancers who haven't the strongest ballet technique because they just won't be able to do my things.

'In America,' he adds, 'it is so lucrative working in musicals that you get really brilliant dancers appearing on Broadway.'

Dougie Squires, top British TV and commercial theatre choreographer, talks about a certain feeling of 'individual competition' among American show dancers who make a regular and highly-paid living out of the musical theatre.

He says: 'I was in New York recently, walking

upstairs to some dance studios to meet a friend for lunch, and suddenly an avalanche of dancers thundered down past me. They'd just spent all morning in heavy rehearsals with Bob Fosse and were all dashing off to do different classes.

'When I got caught up in their wave of enthusiasm it made me feel very inadequate. You see, the competition there is so fierce that they have to work at pressure all the time or they won't stand a chance. But this element of competitiveness among dancers in Britain isn't all that apparent.'

Acquiring a wide range of experience

If British show dancers are not as openly ambitious, in a cut-throat way, as their American colleagues, then this is not because choreographers and teachers in Britain do not do their best to encourage it. They are well aware of the competition that all dancers must face in the commercial theatre.

Bill Drydale, a dancer-choreographer much in demand on stage and in television, has quite definite ideas about what he expects of the dancers he employs. 'A good comprehensive dance training is the obvious requirement,' he says, 'though the next important thing is the acquisition of a wide range of experience.'

This, he emphasises, should involve working with a great number of choreographers, all making different stylistic demands. But the structure of the dance business in Britain usually makes this impossible. For instance, a dancer may become a highly proficient member of one established TV dance group, spending her entire time working very profitably for one choreographer but not actually increasing her range of experience.

In the British commercial theatre, experimental dance appears to be little more than imitating contemporary techniques – although Gillian Lynne and Anthony van Laast, in West End shows like *Cats* and *Song and Dance*, have revealed in their clever choreography what *can* be achieved – and the dancers themselves seem to let their talents go into semi-hibernation between jobs.

Jane Darling, besides being a popular 'featured' dancer on television, is also a teacher working at a number of important dance schools in England. The advice she offers her own students is this: Go to America, to Paris, to Germany or Sweden where the dance world is alive with people experimenting and creating in 'workshops'. There, too, she says, there is a more varied range of dance teachers.

Seasonal work

To their credit, most British dance schools do encourage their pupils to take seasonal work during their training period to gain initial experience. Pantomimes and summer shows inspire the idea of performing, and dancing before an audience can count towards gaining membership to the theatrical union, Equity, without which many or most dance jobs are difficult to come by.

Working in cabaret and the commercial theatre, then, is not for the lazy or weak-hearted. Competition for jobs is as great, if not greater, than competition for places in a modern or classical dance company. An ability to keep trying, no matter what disappoint-ments, is as essential as an ability to catch a choreographer's eye.

Chapter 11

THE TELEVISION DANCER

Laura James is a member of television's offbeat dance group Hot Gossip. She joined the team when she was sixteen, and the first thing choreographer Arlene Phillips did was to dye her hair bright red.

Her elevation to one of the most original and sexy dance groups on television is a classic one. As a shy five-year-old, her parents enrolled her at dancing school to try and 'bring her out'. On the suggestion of a teacher, she continued her training at the nearby Italia Conti stage school.

Laura's first professional job was as an extra in the TV serial *Clayhanger*. Some time later she played an orphan in the original London cast of the musical *Annie*. She then left school to concentrate on dancing – and, six months later, found herself competing with two hundred other girls for a place in Hot Gossip.

She got in, of course.

Apart from dancing on television shows, she also appears with the group in cabaret and pop concerts.

She still can't believe that, after a show, people come up to her and ask for her autograph.

Another member of Hot Gossip, Kim Leeson, offers this advice to would-be television dancers: 'If you're young, the first thing is to get yourself into a good dance school, preferably full time. I think it's important to have a training in classical ballet. Most dancing stems from classical dance, anyway. You can do other classes as well, but I think ballet is a necessity. I'm glad I did it.'

So Kim was a trained dancer before she joined Hot Gossip. 'I started off by doing ballet classes once a week from the age of three,' she explains. 'I then auditioned for the Royal Ballet School and stayed there a couple of years.

'But I wasn't the right shape. You have to be ultra-slim for ballet. So I moved to a special school where I did ballet, jazz, singing – everything.'

Importance of personality

An all-round training in all forms of dance, including modern and jazz tap, is therefore vital to the girl or boy hoping to break into the competitive world of television. Personality, too, is important. Directors are more likely to be impressed by a 'personality girl' than by a negative applicant who may technically be a much better dancer.

It may surprise many people to know, in fact, that top choreographers like Lionel Blair, Flick Colby, Norman Maen, Gillian Lynne, Nigel Lythgoe, Arlene Phillips, Dougie Squires and Irving Davies are not looking specifically for a girl with a superb technique and breath-taking *arabesques*, because these qualities

105

are not likely to be seen or appreciated in the dynamic, hurly-burly world of television dancing.

Dougie Squires, who started television's famous dancing group The Young Generation, says: 'Personality is most important in the small groups of girls seen in television shows. It is far less important in the larger teams engaged for West End musicals.

'I like distinctive dancers on television, girls who stand a chance of being picked out as individuals. It is good to hear a viewer exclaim, "I like the blonde!" That means the girl has made a personal impact and the viewer is showing more interest than he would in a line of girls who all look alike.'

Fast learners essential

Television dancers must also be fast learners, able to pick up steps in a routine immediately.

'No television dance director,' adds Squires, 'dare take the risk of engaging slow studiers when he himself is always working to a rushed schedule.'

Height for a girl in television is not very important. What is essential is a good figure, striking looks and a quick brain. Smartness in appearance is a must.

It is also vital that the television dancer has another string to her bow. Very few dancers can rely *entirely* on television for an income. Cabaret is an ideal alternative source of income, because the work is similar and the hours do not clash.

Television wins new audiences for dance

There can be little doubt that television's many dance groups, led by Hot Gossip and Legs & Co., have brought dance – and especially modern dance – to the attention of a public which might otherwise have shown complete indifference to it. Arlene Phillips, founder and choreographer of Hot Gossip, is certain of one thing: 'People who would normally never leave their homes to see anything, let alone modern dance, come to see us at "live" events because of the television coverage.'

She then explains: 'We attract a totally new audience to what is in essence a very sexy, modern dance group. And although we do commercial numbers I also put in serious work, so that audiences are not just seeing wildly "suggestive" dances in outlandish costumes.'

In common with most television dance directors, she is a great admirer of American modern dance choreographers. There is a slickness about their work which is generally looked up to. Alvin Ailey is an especial favourite. The worlds of jazz and modern dance, and classical ballet, all find their way into Miss Phillips' fantastic choreography – including the dances she created for such films as *The Fan*, *Can't Stop the Music* and *Annie*.

'People all over the world are in love with the Gossip girls, and the boys, too,' says Arlene Phillips. 'Hot Gossip are fit, energetic, supple, clean and beautiful. They're wholesome as well as sexy, and people respond to that.'

Need to study new techniques

Claims that television dancers are overpaid, adds Miss Phillips, are simply not true. 'They earn less than anyone in show business,' she reveals. 'Hot Gossip are the highest-paid dance group in Britain, yes, but that's because people want to see us and, anyway, we've worked for it.

'If you could see the boys and girls coming off stage at the end of their cabaret act, collapsing in the wings, being given oxygen in Mexico City, taking classes in the morning after travelling back through the night from a show, you would see they earn every penny.

'These dancers have trained hard for years. They're constantly studying new techniques, rehearsing new routines, fighting to make sure they stay way ahead of their growing army of imitators. Oh yes, they *work* for their money.'

Disappointments – and glamour

In fact, dancing on television involves as much discipline and dedication as dancing in ballet or modern dance. Time is always very scarce, and dancers have to learn their routines quickly while trying to fit in rehearsals with those of the stars of the shows they are appearing in, such as Twiggy, Rolf Harris or Liza Minnelli.

But, despite the toughness and persistence required just to survive in such a fiercely competitive business, and despite all the hard work, the frustrations, disappointments and long hours, the life of the television dancer is without question an enviable one. It is always full of adventure, challenge and, yes, glamour.

Chapter 12

DANCE OF THE FUTURE?

We have seen how theatrical dance began in the royal courts of Europe and developed into the form we know as classical ballet. We have looked at today's modern dance, at jazz and tap dancing, and at the dancing to be found in the commercial theatre, in cabaret and on television.

Yet anyone who goes to performances of dance will know that it is not easy to label everything he or she sees. In all forms of dance, at any one time, there is a certain amount of experimental work going on which can only be described as 'odd' or 'extraordinary', performances that fall outside the customary area of modern or classic dance.

I've seen dances created for a fork-lift truck and dances in art galleries where the audience has to take part by walking under enormous billowing plastic sheeting and then get to their seats by going through a sort of maze. I've seen dancers hanging from walls and ceilings and spending whole performances banging pots and pans and ripping loaves of bread to pieces and sticking the fragments in the mouths of the bewildered audience.

In the dances of the future, incidentally, the audience is often required to work as much as watch others working. They have a tough deal.

I've seen dancers become human pogo sticks. The performers in America's gymnastic, acrobatic, athletic Pilobolus Dance Theatre are very good at this sort of thing. In some other works they pile upon, around and underneath each other like dedicated limpets and create a continual flow of funny shapes which are neither human, animal or vegetable (the company itself is named after a fungus).

In New York I've found myself sitting in a studio-loft watching two male dancers spray shaving cream on their teeth, while two girls, one in a maternity smock and the other simply gift-wrapped in cellophane, watched with disinterest.

Also in New York I've been present while Steve Paxton – inventor of a dance-form called 'contact improvisation' – unfolded a transparent plastic bag into which he crawled. His partner, Yvonne Rainer, using a vacuum cleaner, then inflated it while Paxton balanced inside. They deflated it and Paxton crawled out. All this potty – and dangerous – behaviour took close on half an hour to happen.

In company with packed out houses at Sadler's Wells in London I've sat amazed while, in Glen Tetley's *Imaginary Film*, one of the girls with Nederlands Dans Theater put on an evening gown and roller-skates and brandished a revolver. Graeme Murphy, artistic director of the Sydney Dance Com-

110

pany, has earned quite a reputation for being 'controversial'; for example, in his version of Ravel's *Daphnis and Chloë*, Cupid rides a skateboard and nymphs arrive on roller-skates.

Where will it all end? Not so long ago Britain's Another Dance Group was the first dance company in this country to become seriously involved in choreography by computer. John Lansdown's *Moving*, for instance, plotted out a framework within which the dancers could perform a series of instant improvisations.

The main thing about a great deal of experimental dance is that the movements all look like things which an untrained dancer might be able to do (although, quite likely, not as engagingly). Many experimentalists have developed a way of dance that enjoys doing the common, everyday actions of life. The dancers mill about, tussle, huddle, scramble, walk, skip, turn somersaults, carry packages, trays, and each other, nudge in crowded groups, break into runs, hop, hobble, pick up books, bounce tennis balls, and balance on a bar.

But this sort of behaviour, as you might expect, does not appeal to everybody – often not even to those in the profession. Robert North, director of the Ballet Rambert, describes much of today's modern dance as 'arid' and says there is 'a real desert of modern dance' which infuriates him.

He says, surprisingly, that 'the dance explosion, especially in America, has not been in modern dance: it is in disco dancing and in classical ballet'.

'In the last twenty years,' he adds, 'we've gone through a strange period in dance. We've thrown out music to begin with, and then we've thrown out real dance coordination and substituted "New Dance" co-ordination (see page 39), which is really an excuse for bad co-ordination.

'But I don't think we can afford to throw out anything; instead we should add it all on. What I love about dancing is that you can go deeper and deeper into it. It is actually growing all the time through all the different people who feed it.'

A merging of ideas and influences

And as dance continues to grow, it will become more and more difficult to make clear distinctions between the two styles. There will be a merging of ideas and influences, and indeed it is already happening. Like plants in a gardener's greenhouse, ballet and modern dance have been cross-fertilised: we see it clearly in the productions of Alvin Ailey, Glen Tetley, Hans van Manen, Robert North, David Bintley, Paul Taylor, Christopher Bruce, Barry Moreland, Jiří Kylián, Jerome Robbins, Twyla Tharp, and many others.

The fact that some principal dancers of the Royal Ballet have worked with the London Contemporary Dance Theatre, as performers and choreographers, and that major modern dance choreographers like Robert North and Christopher Bruce have worked with the Royal Ballet in London, is a major step forward. It is proof that classical and modern artforms are no longer working against each other but together as allies in dance.

As for *today*'s new breed of dance-makers, they are bringing to ballet some of the most vibrantly exciting aspects of the modern or Martha Graham school. It is no longer unusual to see a ballet dancer droop and convulse, fall to the floor, spin on a non-vertical or changing axis, beat and stamp with his feet, and dance off beat – the ballets of Kenneth MacMillan, for instance, are full of such things.

New world of possibilities

The great Russian superstar of classical ballet, Mikhail Baryshnikov, says he owes a great deal to modern dance for 'opening up' his own classical style. It occurred when American modern dance choreographer Twyla Tharp cast him in her *Deuce Coupe*, a piece inspired by surfing, open sports cars and beach parties. It is performed to a medley of songs by the Beach Boys.

Says Baryshnikov: 'When I first saw Twyla Tharp all I could think of was, "You probably have to be born in America to do it". This whole mixture of classical ballet, jazz, tap, social dancing needs a special technique and a special accent that seemed so foreign to me.

'But it was obvious to me from the beginning that her work was serious and had a highly developed, *willed* style. Seeing her ballets, and performing in one of them, opened up for me a whole new world of possibilities for the use of classical ballet steps.'

Other dancers in ballet are also finding that performing in works outside their usual area of dance is liberating them in a thrilling new way. This is why Rudolf Nureyev decided to appear with the modern dance companies of people like Martha Graham, Murray Louis and Paul Taylor: to do so 'opens up' his own particular style.

Modern dance is bringing ballet down to earth, and the influence of ballet is helping to make modern dance less earthbound. Cross-fertilisation is at work . . . and is working. Modern dance used to be noted for the 'obscure' or baffling nature of its productions, but more and more people associated with the artform are beginning to realise that the alternative to story-ballets like *Giselle* or *Swan Lake* is not necessarily a diet of abstract works without heart, humour or common sense.

'If what the modern artist has to say is important,' insists Robert North, 'then he should make it *understandable*.'

His English modern dancer-choreographer wife, Janet Smith, says simply: 'A modern dance performance should be magical, mysterious, *but not mystifying*.'

Tomorrow's dance

Modern dance and jazz dancing has entered our lives on a scale as never before, thanks largely to television series such as *Fame* and groups like Hot Gossip and Legs & Co. and the numerous 'backing' dancers who bring many a light entertainment show to life.

Even pop singers like Kate Bush, Sheena Easton, Adam Ant and Toyah have jazz/modern dance choreographers like Norman Maen, Anthony van Laast and Nigel Lythgoe working away in the background to make them look good. In such a *visual* age, a time of television and video cassettes, it is no longer enough for pop singers to just sing.

They must be 'packaged' or 'sold' within the context of a fabulous dance routine. They must be choreographed, perhaps in a sequence comprising several dancers. They must move, often in a style that combines dramatic gestures and freakish dance. They must be *seen*.

Offbeat movement, especially for people like Toyah and Kate Bush, is as important to their general image as the music they sing. Movement and song cannot be separated. Kate Bush, quite simply, would not be Kate Bush at a live concert without the services of a modern dance choreographer – the person who remains in the shadows.

And today in Britain and elsewhere there are more modern dance artists giving concerts than at any other time in the artform's history. Annual festivals of modern dance are held up and down the country. What they perform is not necessarily for today – it is for tomorrow.

As Christopher Bruce reflects, 'There will always be an audience for classical ballet, a need for classical training. But you must have experience of contemporary training to create for the future.'

In the end it is what will keep serious theatrical dance alive. It is what audiences, you and I, will demand.

Fourth Step

A GUIDE TO DANCES, PERFORMERS, CHOREOGRAPHERS, COMPANIES AND SCHOOLS

Chapter 13

DANCES TO SEE

Unlike classical ballet, which hopes its productions will remain in the repertory for many years, new productions staged for most modern dance and experimental dance companies are usually intended to last for little more than a season or two. This is because the main interest of these companies (especially the smaller ones) lies in the process of creation, and in order to produce a steady flow of new works it is necessary to make room for them by discarding most of the existing ones. But some dances *do* survive, including those listed in the selection below.

(NOTE: *ch*. means 'choreography by'; *m*. 'music by'; *f.p.* signifies the company which gave the work its first performance, plus where and in what year. They are all one-act works unless otherwise stated.)

Appalachian Spring: ch. Martha Graham; *m*. Aaron Copland; *f.p*. Martha Graham Dance Company, Washington, 1944. A recently-married young couple set up house in the puritanical atmosphere of America's pioneer days.

As Time Goes By: ch. Twyla Tharp; *m.* Franz Joseph Haydn; *f.p.* City Center Joffrey Ballet, New York, 1973. The Austrian composer's 'Farewell Symphony' is used in a plotless dance that seems to wave goodbye to certain customs of classic ballet – and says hello to modern dance.

Aureole: ch. Paul Taylor; *m.* George Frideric Handel; *f.p.* Paul Taylor Dance Company, New London, Connecticut, 1962. Beautifully made series of lyrical dances with delicious moments of humour.

The Bix Pieces: ch. Twyla Tharp; *m.* Bix Beiderbecke; *f.p.* Twyla Tharp and Dancers, New York, 1972. Captures in dance a flavour of 1920s and 1930s jazz and includes visions of ballroom dances, chorus-girl routines, baton-twirling parades and tap dancing.

Cave of the Heart: ch. Martha Graham; *m.* Samuel Barber; *f.p.* Martha Graham Dance Company, New York, 1946. Based on the story of the legendary sorceress Medea who helped Jason, leader of the Argonauts, win the Golden Fleece on his promising to marry her.

Cell: ch. Robert Cohan; *m.* Ronald Lloyd; *f.p.* London Contemporary Dance Theatre, London, 1969. An abstract look at how people today sometimes feel 'hemmed in' by the demands which society places on them.

Clytemnestra: ch. Martha Graham; *m.* Halim El-Dabh; *f.p.* Martha Graham Dance Company, New York, 1958. The choreographer's (and modern dance's) first evening-long work, comprising two acts with prologue and epilogue, and based on the three *Oresteia* plays by the ancient Greek dramatist Aeschylus. Clytemnestra ponders her eternal fate in the Underworld while the gods sit in judgment on her past sins.

Deuce Coupe: ch. Twyla Tharp; *m.* Beach Boys; *f.p.* City Center Joffrey Ballet with Twyla Tharp and Dancers, New York, 1973. Modern and classical steps are explored separately, but at the same time, until the two styles gradually merge into an explosion of good humoured dance.

Diversion of Angels: ch. Martha Graham; *m.* Norman Dello Joio; *f.p.* Martha Graham Dance Company, New London, Connecticut, 1948. Explores in lyrical dances the joys and sadness of youth, and the pain and pleasure of first love.

Eight Jelly Rolls: ch. Twyla Tharp; *m.* Jelly Roll Morton; *f.p.* Twyla Tharp and Dancers, New York, 1971. A tribute to black jazz music and a happy-go-lucky celebration of the 'good times' of the Roaring Twenties.

Embrace Tiger and Return to Mountain: ch. Glen Tetley; *m.* Morton Subotnick; *f.p.* Ballet Rambert, London, 1968. Inspired by a system of shadow-boxing, known as *T'ai-Chi*, developed by the Chinese in the sixth century.

Earrand into the Maze: ch. Martha Graham; *m.* Gian Carlo Menotti; *f.p.* Martha Graham Dance Company, New York, 1947. A version of the famous myth of the Greek hero Theseus and his journey into the

121

labyrinth to kill the monstrous Minotaur – here told in terms of a woman and of her conquest of a so-called Creature of Fear.

Field Figures: ch. Glen Tetley; *m.* Karlheinz Stockhausen; *f.p.* Royal Ballet touring company (now Sadler's Wells Royal Ballet), Nottingham, 1970. An extended abstract-style duet which is broken off at frequent intervals by five other dancers.

. . . for those who die as cattle: ch. Christopher Bruce; no music; *f.p.* Ballet Rambert, London, 1972. Deals with the horror of war and death; the title is a quotation from the English poet Wilfred Owen, himself killed (aged twenty-five) in the First World War.

Green Table, The: ch. Kurt Jooss; *m.* Frederick (Fritz) Cohen; *f.p.* Ballets Jooss, Paris, 1932. Dance-drama showing the futility of war, beginning and ending with the pointless discussions of politicians around the green table, and watched over throughout by the menacing figure of Death.

How to Pass, Kick, Fall and Run: ch. Merce Cunningham; *m.* John Cage (reading from two of his books); *f.p.* Merce Cunningham Dance Company, Chicago, 1965. A playful, frisky, humorous piece in which the cast of three women and three men embark on a series of earnest games, like jumping, skipping and playing 'tag'.

Huescape: ch. Louis Falco; *m.* Pierre Henry, Pierre Schaeffer, Jacques Lasry, and Bernard Bascet; *f.p.* Louis Falco and Featured Dancers, Lee, Massachusetts, 1968. Explores the emotional relationship of a woman and two men.

Hunter of Angels: ch. Robert Cohan; *m.* Bruno Maderna; *f.p.* Robert Cohan and Dancers, New York, 1967. Based on the Old Testament story of the twin brothers Jacob and Esau.

Icarus: ch. Lucas Hoving; *m.* Chin-Ichi Matushita; *f.p.* Lucas Hoving and Dancers, 92nd Street YM-YWHA, New York, 1964. Inspired by the Greek myth in which Icarus, granted the power of flight, flies too near the sun, thereby melting the wax with which his wings are secured and sending him crashing to his death: the dance's moral is that people should not soar beyond their abilities.

Imago: ch. and *m.* Alwin Nikolais; *f.p.* Alwin Nikolais Dance Company, Hartford, Connecticut, 1963. The choreographer's first full-length work, sub-titled *The City Curious*, comprising a kaleidoscope of colours, patterns, shapes, forms, movements, costumes and sounds in eleven episodes.

Junk Dances: ch. Murray Louis; *m.* medley of popular and operatic music; *f.p.* Murray Louis and Company, New York, 1964. A funny send-up of married life, performed to music ranging from *Bye, Bye, Blackbird* to Brahms' *Variations on a Theme of Haydn*.

Laborintus: ch. Glen Tetley; *m.* Luciano Berio; *f.p.* Royal Ballet, London, 1972. Life on earth as depicted in the twistings and turnings of a maze where the only way out leads to death.

Moor's Pavane, The: ch. José Limón; *m.* Henry Purcell, *f.p.* José Limón Dance Company, New London, Connecticut, 1949. One of the best-known danced accounts of a Shakespeare play. It is based on the tragic jealousies found in *Othello*.

Night Journey: ch. Martha Graham; *m.* William Schumann; *f.p.* Martha Graham Dance Company, Cambridge, Massachusetts, 1947. Based on the legend of the Greek hero Oedipus, who, unknowingly, killed his father and married his own mother, Jocasta – and it is through her eyes that the whole drama is seen in 'flashback'.

Pierrot Lunaire: ch. Glen Tetley; *m.* Arnold Schoenberg; *f.p.* Glen Tetley and Dancers, New York, 1962. Serious dance-drama inspired by the early pantomime characters of the white-faced, gloomy Pierrot, the romantic Columbine and the scheming Brighella.

Revelations: ch. Alvin Ailey; *m.* spirituals sung by a choir; *f.p.* Alvin Ailey American Dance Theatre, New York, 1960. Ailey's most popular work. It explores in dance the emotions of black American religious music, showing sorrow, shame, hope, exhilaration and joy.

Rite of Spring: ch. Richard Alston; *m.* Igor Stravinsky (not the usual orchestral score but the composer's four-handed version for piano); *f.p.* Ballet Rambert, London, 1981. Dance-drama based on the theme of a fertility rite during which a girl is sacrificed.

Rooms: ch. Anna Sokolow; *m*. Kenyon Hopkins; *f.p*. Soloists, New York, 1955. Deals with loneliness in a big city.

Seraphic Dialogue: ch. Martha Graham; *m*. Norman Dello Joio; *f.p*. Martha Graham Dance Company, New York, 1955. Drama about Joan of Arc who, as she is about to be received at the gate of Heaven into the communion of saints, sees herself as Maid, Warrior, and Martyr.

Summerspace: ch. Merce Cunningham; *m*. Morton Feldman; *f.p*. Merce Cunningham Dance Company, New London, Connecticut, 1958. A plotless work about changing tempos in which the dancers resemble camouflaged winged insects in a summer landscape.

Tent: ch. and *m*. Alwin Nikolais; *f.p*. Alwin Nikolais Dance Company, Tampa, Florida, 1968. A large circular white tent assumes a life of its own.

Three Epitaphs: ch. Paul Taylor; *m*. American folk music played on brass-band instruments; *f.p*. Paul Taylor Dance Company, New York, 1956. Comic dance with the performers' bodies and faces completely covered in coal-black costumes, with metallic 'eyes'.

Troy Game: ch. Robert North; *m*. Bob Downes; *f.p*. London Contemporary Dance Theatre, London, 1974. Young men at play, each one trying to outdo the other in what is really an exploration of male athleticism and strength.

Winterbranch: ch. Merce Cunningham; *m.* LaMonte Young; *f.p.* Merce Cunningham Dance Company, Hartford, Connecticut, 1964. A plotless ballet, one of the choreographer's most intriguing, with stage lighting ranging from pitch darkness to glaring brightness, and a score that is sometimes played so loud it seems to deafen the spectator.

Chapter 14

DANCERS AND CHOREOGRAPHERS

Alvin Ailey: American dancer, choreographer, teacher and ballet director. Born Rogers, Texas, 1931. Formed his own Alvin Ailey American Dance Theatre in 1958. His many dances include *Blues Suite*, *Quintet*, *Hermit Songs*, *The River* and his immensely popular *Revelations*

Richard Alston: English dancer and choreographer. Born Stoughton, Sussex, 1948. Former art student. Founded own company, Strider, 1972. Later joined London Contemporary Dance Theatre. Resident choreographer of Ballet Rambert since 1980. His dances include *Tiger Balm*, *Blue Schubert Fragments*, *Rainbow Ripples* and *Rite of Spring*.

Talley Beatty: American dancer and choreographer. Born New Orleans, about 1923. Danced in the ethnic dance companies of Katherine Dunham and Pearl

Primus. His unique Negro and jazz dances include *The Road of the Phoebe Snow*, *Come and Get the Beauty of it Hot* and *Cathedral of Heaven*.

Micha Bergese: German dancer, choreographer and ballet director. Born Munich, 1946. Trained originally as a 'cellist. Now lives and works in Britain. Member of the London Contemporary Dance Theatre for many years (later as associate choreographer) before forming his own Mantis Dance Company in 1980. His dances include *Hinterland*, *The Act of Waiting*, *Scene Shift* and *Nema*.

Carolyn Brown: American dancer and choreographer. Born Fitchburg, Massachusetts, 1927. Star of the Merce Cunningham Dance Company, New York, 1953–73, collaborating with Cunningham and composer John Cage on dozens of works. Her own dances include *Balloon*, *As I Remember It* and *House Party*.

Christopher Bruce: English dancer and choreographer. Born Leicester, 1945. Finest modern dancer of his generation. Associated with the Ballet Rambert since 1963 (he is now the company's associate choreographer), his most notable performance being Pierrot in Glen Tetley's *Pierrot Lunaire*. His own dances include *There Was a Time*, *for those who die as cattle*, *Unfamiliar Playground* and (with Lindsay Kemp) the full-length *Cruel Garden*.

John Butler: American dancer and choreographer. Born Memphis, 1920. Danced with the Martha Graham company in New York and with his own group. His many dances include *Carmina Burana*, *After Eden* and *Portrait of Billie*.

Lucinda Childs: American dancer, teacher and choreographer. Born New York, 1940. One of the great practitioners of experimental dance in America.

Robert Cohan: American dancer, choreographer, teacher and ballet director. Born New York, 1925. For many years a member of the Martha Graham Dance Company, New York, and one of Graham's regular partners. Artistic director (1967–83) of the London Contemporary Dance School and (1969–83) of the London Contemporary Dance Theatre, which he helped to form. His many dances include *Cell*, *Hunter of Angels*, full-evening *Stages*, *Waterless Method of Swimming Instruction* and the full-length *Dances of Love and Death*. His pioneering work has transformed the LCDT into the foremost modern dance company in Europe.

Merce Cunningham: American dancer, choreographer, teacher and ballet director. Born Centralia, Washington, 1919. After dancing with the Martha Graham company in New York, he formed (in 1952) his own Merce Cunningham Dance Company, now one of the world's greatest modern groups, to dance exclusively his own works. Works in close collaboration with the experimental composer John Cage. His numerous dances include *Summerspace*, *Field Dances*, *How to Pass, Kick, Fall and Run*, *Winterbranch* and *Squaregame*.

Siobhan Davies: English dancer, choreographer and ballet director. Born London, 1950. Real name: Sue Davies. Former art student. Associated with London Contemporary Dance Theatre since 1971, as leading dancer and associate choreographer. Also director of her own dance group. Her dances include *Pilot*, *Diary* and *Free Setting*.

Isadora Duncan: American dancer, teacher and pioneer of 'free' dance. Born (of Irish parents) San Francisco, 1878; died Nice, France, 1927. Disliking the artificial nature of ballet she tried to restore simplicity, naturalness and true emotion to dancing. With the English stage designer Edward Gordon Craig she devised productions based on architectural forms, drapery and lighting effects with dancers dressed in simple Greek tunics and usually bare-footed. Her importance lies in the fact that she influenced modern choreographers from the Russian Mikhail Fokine to the American Martha Graham.

Katherine Dunham: American dancer, teacher, choreographer and ballet director. Born Chicago, 1912. At her peak was one of the most sought-after choreographers for dances of a distinctive Afro-Cuban-American style.

Louis Falco: American dancer, choreographer and ballet director. Born New York, 1942. Formed his own company in 1968 and began to create dances, including *Caviar*, *Sleepers* and *Tutti-frutti*.

Loie Fuller: American dancer. Born Fullersburg, Illinois, 1862, died Paris, 1928. Self-taught performer whose concerts made great use of voluminous silk materials illuminated with gorgeous colours from lighting concealed under the stage. Was hugely popular. Her best-known numbers were *Serpentine Dance* and *Fire Dance*.

Martha Graham: American dancer, choreographer, teacher and director of her own company, formed in 1929. Born Allegheny, Pennsylvania, 1894. Founded the Martha Graham School of Dance in New York in 1927, which has since become the major training ground and influence for modern dance as it is generally recognised today. She calls her productions 'dance plays', most of which explore the myths and legends of Europe and the United States. Created more than a hundred and sixty dances, among them *Appalachian Spring*, *Cave of the Heart*, *Night Journey*, the full-length *Clytemnestra*, *Lucifer* (created for Margot Fonteyn and Rudolf Nureyev) and *The Owl and the Pussycat*.

Ann Halprin: American dancer, teacher and choreographer. Born Winnetka, Illinois, 1920. A pioneer of the dance 'happening', often using up to a hundred of her students. One of the first choreographers to use nudity in modern dance. Yvonne Rainer, James Waring, Trisha Brown and Meredith Monk are among her famous pupils.

Erick Hawkins: American dancer, teacher and choreographer. Born Trinidad, Colorado, 1909. Dancer with the Martha Graham company in New York, 1938–51, then formed his own company. Created many dances (often in collaboration with the composer Lucia Dlugoszewski and the sculptor Ralph Dorazio), including *Classic Kite Tails* and *Here and Now with Watchers*.

Hanya Holm: German-American dancer, teacher and choreographer. Born Worms-am-Rhein, 1898. In Germany she studied with the great Swiss composer and teacher Emile Jaques Dalcroze and with the German dance pioneer Mary Wigman. Later in America she evolved a system of teaching which made her one of the architects of the modern dance movement, her former pupils numbering such modern dance 'greats' of today as Alwin Nikolais, Don Redlich and Glen Tetley.

Lester Horton: American dancer, choreographer and teacher. Born Indianapolis, 1906; died Los Angeles, 1953. Especially famous for his teaching methods and for his many (now famous) pupils, including Alvin Ailey, Bella Lewitsky, Carmen De Lavallade, Joyce Trisler and James Truitte, all of whom have made a notable contribution to American modern dance. His best-known dance is *The Beloved*.

Doris Humphrey: American dancer, choreographer and teacher. Born Oak Park, Illinois, 1895; died New York, 1958. One of the pioneers of American modern dance. Formed her own group and was the partner for many years of the great American dancer Charles Weidman.

Kurt Jooss: German dancer, choreographer, teacher and ballet director. Born Wasseralfingen, 1901; died 1980. Formed famous school in Essen, Germany, and became director of the local company, for which he created his most famous work, *The Green Table*. The company later moved to Britain, then to the United States, before returning to Germany. One of the first major choreographers to successfully combine modern and classical dance in his works.

Cliff Keuter: American dancer, choreographer and ballet director. Born Boise, Idaho, 1940. Performed in the dance companies of Helen Tamiris and Paul Taylor before forming his own group, for which he has created many dances. His works include *Amazing Grace*, *Table* and *Sunday Papers*.

Anthony van Laast: English dancer and choreographer. Born Sussex, 1951. Performed with London Contemporary Dance Theatre, 1971–79, and now teaches and choreographs for films, television and commercial theatre. His works for modern dance include *Outside-In* and *Just Before*.

Pearl Lang: American dancer, choreographer and teacher. Born Chicago, 1922. For many years one of the stars of the Martha Graham Dance Company and the first performer to take over roles created by Graham. Formed her own company in 1952. Her many dances include the full-length *The Possessed*.

José Limón: Mexican-American dancer, choreographer, teacher and ballet director. Born Culiacán, Mexico, 1908; died Flemington, New Jersey, 1972. After dancing with the modern dance company of Charles Weidman and Doris Humphrey he formed his own company (which still continues in New York), for which he created his best-known work, *The Moor's Pavane*. A giant among modern dance personalities.

Murray Louis: American dancer, choreographer, teacher and ballet director. Born New York, 1926. Closely associated with the Alwin Nikolais Dance Theatre, New York, 1948–69. Has choreographed professionally from 1953, often for his own group, the

Murray Louis Dance Company. His most popular work is *Junk Dances*.

William Louther: American dancer, choreographer, teacher and ballet director. Born New York, 1942. Danced with the modern dance companies of Alvin Ailey, Donald McKayle and Martha Graham in the United States and in Britain with the London Contemporary Dance Theatre. One of the finest dancers of his generation. His dances include *In the Playground of the Zodiac* and *Vesalii Icones*.

Lar Lubovitch: American dancer and choreographer. Born Chicago, 1943. Appeared with many modern dance companies before turning to choreography. His dances include *Whirligogs*, *Considering the Lilies* and *Marimba*.

Meredith Monk: American dancer and choreographer. Born New York, 1942. One of the pioneers of American experimental dance. Her dances usually take place in non-theatrical settings, such as museums and art galleries.

Alwin Nikolais: American dancer, choreographer, teacher, composer, designer and ballet director. Born Southington, Connecticut, 1912. Directed his own company, the Alwin Nikolais Dance Theatre, since 1948. His spectacular productions are choreographed, designed, lit and scored musically by Nikolais into a kaleidoscope of visual magic. His many works include *Imago*, *Tent*, *Cross-Fade* and *Tribe*. There is no dance-maker like him; he is unique.

Robert North: American dancer, choreographer and ballet director. Born Charleston, South Carolina, 1945. Real name: Robert Dodson. Danced with Martha Graham Dance Company in New York and the London Contemporary Dance Theatre. As associate choreographer with LCDT began creating dances, which include *Reflections*, *Death and the Maiden* and the popular *Troy Games*. In 1981 he became artistic director of the Ballet Rambert.

Steve Paxton: American dancer, teacher and choreographer. Born Phoenix, Arizona, 1939. Performed with Merce Cunningham and other modern dance companies in New York. Later turned to teaching and choreography and devising a system of dance known as 'contact improvisation'. A pioneer of theatrical non-dance movement: walking, crawling, standing still.

Yvonne Rainer: American dancer, teacher and choreographer. Born San Francisco, 1934. Danced in many modern dance companies, including New York's pioneering experimental group Judson Dance Workshop. One of the dance world's most enthusiastic rebels. In her dances she makes great use of film. Her most famous dance, which she has taught to hundreds of students, is *Trio A*.

Dame Marie Rambert: Polish-British dancer, teacher and ballet director. Born Warsaw, 1888; died London, 1982. Real name: Cyvia Rambam. From her classical-based Ballet Rambert company, formed in London in 1930, there emerged in 1966 the smaller modern-dance Ballet Rambert we know today – and now one of Europe's major contemporary-style groups. American choreographer Glen Tetley was encouraged by the company, which in turn received a vibrant new identity from his works as well as from other American choreographers like Anna Sokolow and Cliff Keuter, and from its own Christopher Bruce, Richard Alston and Robert North.

Ruth St Denis: American dancer, teacher and choreographer. Born New Jersey, 1877; died Hollywood, 1968. Real name: Ruth Dennis. After appearing as a featured dancer in the commercial theatre she married dancer Ted Shawn and together they formed (in 1915) the Denishawn School of Dance in Los Angeles. From the school and its company arose America's first platform of modern dance. Like Isadora Duncan, her dancing and dances were inspired by Oriental art; her art in turn inspired the careers of such modern dance performers as Martha Graham, Doris Humphrey and Charles Weidman, all of whom began their careers at Denishawn.

Ted Shawn: American dancer, teacher and choreographer. Born Kansas City, 1891; died Orlando, Florida, 1972. Real name: Edwin Meyers. (See also 'Ruth St Denis' entry above.) His masculine teaching styles did much to overcome prejudice against male dancing in America. A farm he bought in 1933, Jacob's Pillow, became the home of the world-famous Jacob's Pillow Dance Festival, which continues to this day.

Anna Sokolow: American dancer, choreographer, teacher and ballet director. Born Hartford, Connecticut, 1912, of Polish parentage. Danced with Martha Graham's New York company for several years, later forming a number of her own groups, and founding (in 1939) Mexico's first modern dance company. Her many dances include *Rooms*, *Dreams* and *Steps of Silence*.

Paul Taylor: American dancer, choreographer and ballet director. Born Pittsburgh, Pennsylvania, 1930. Performed with the modern dance companies of Merce Cunningham, Pearl Lang and Martha Graham, and later with his own Paul Taylor Dance Company (formed 1954). *Three Epitaphs*, *Aureole*, *Scudorama* and *Cloven Kingdom* are among the most popular of his many dances.

Glen Tetley: American dancer, choreographer and ballet director. Born Cleveland, Ohio, 1926. Former medical student. Danced in musicals, classical and modern dance companies, before taking charge of his own dance company and that of the Nederlands Dans Theater and the Stuttgart Ballet. This varied background of commercial theatre, ballet and modern dance has come together in one satisfying whole in his dances (known as 'Alto-Classicism'). These include his masterpiece, *Pierrot Lunaire* and *Field Figures*, *Laborintus*, *Greening* and the full-length *Tempest*.

Twyla Tharp: American dancer, choreographer and ballet director. Born Portland, Indiana, 1942. Danced with Paul Taylor's New York company before forming her own group and later turning to choreography. Her dances include *Eight Jelly Rolls*, *Deuce Coupe*, *As Time Goes By* and *Push Comes to Shove*.

Charles Weidman: American dancer, choreographer, teacher and ballet director. Born Lincoln, Nebraska, 1901; died New York, 1975. Danced with the Denishawn company (see 'Ruth St Denis' entry) before forming his own company with dancer Doris Humphrey, which ran from 1928 to 1945. He and Humphrey established the 'fall and recovery' technique that is such an important part of today's modern dance. José Limón and Bob Fosse were among his now-famous dancer-choreographer pupils.

Mary Wigman: German dancer, choreographer and teacher. Born Hanover, 1886; died Berlin, 1973. Real name: Marie Wiegmann. Germany's most famous modern dancer and a pioneer of the Modern European or Central European style of dance, which spread to America through such pupils as Hanya Holm, who in turn influenced such pupils as Alwin Nikolais and Glen Tetley.

Chapter 15

FURTHER INFORMATION

1. SCHOOLS WHERE MODERN DANCE IS TAUGHT

Doreen Bird College of Theatre Dance, Birkbeck Centre, Birkbeck Road, Sidcup, Kent DA14 4DE. Tel. 01-300 6004.

Guildford School of Acting and Drama Dance Education, Millbrook, Guildford, Surrey. Tel. 0483 71722.

Laban Centre for Movement and Dance, University of London, Goldsmiths' College, New Cross, London, SE14 6NW. Tel. 01-691 5750 & 692 0211.

London Contemporary Dance School, The Place, 17 Dukes Road, London, WC1H 9AB. Tel. 01-387 0161.

London Studio Centre, 5 Tavistock Place, London, WC1H 9SS. Tel. 01-388 5850.

Stella Mann School of Dancing, 343a Finchley Road, London, NW3. Tel. 01-435 9317.

Rambert Academy, West London Institute of Higher

Education, Gordon House, 300 St Margaret's Road, Twickenham, Middx. TW1 1PT. Tel. 01-891 0121.

Rambert School of Ballet, The Place, 17 Dukes Road, London, WC1H 9AB. Tel. 01-387 0161.

Tozer School of Dance and Drama, Adelphi Dance Club, 159 Wollaton Street, Nottingham. Tel. 0602 411625 & 250419.

Urdang Academy of Ballet and Performing Arts, 20–22 Shelton Street, London, WC2H 9JJ. Tel. 01-836 5709.

2. MODERN DANCE COMPANIES

Ballet Rambert, 94 Chiswick High Road, London W4 1SH. Tel. 01-995 4246.

Basic Space Dance Theatre, 45 Queen Street, Edinburgh. Tel. 031-225 4857.

Rosemary Butcher Dance Company, 40 Alderville Road, London, SW6. Tel. 01-731 5145.

Dance Experience for Children (now merged with the London Contemporary Dance Experience)

Dance Theatre London, c/o Flat 1, Stirling Mansions, 12 Canfield Gardens, London NW6 3JJ. Tel. 01-328 8375.

Dancework, 7 Windermere Road, Muswell Hill, London, N10 2RD. Tel. 01-444 8183.

English Dance Theatre, The Arts Centre, Vane Terrace, Darlington DL3 7AX. Tel. 0325 483260.

Extempory Dance Theatre, 5 Dryden Street, London, WC2E 9NW. Tel. 01-240 2430.

Jumpers, c/o Caricature Theatre, Station Terrace, Cardiff CF1 4EW. Tel. 0222 374845.

London Contemporary Dance Theatre, The Place, 17

Dukes Road, London, WC1H 9AB. Tel. 01-387 0161. (Parent company of London Contemporary Dance Experience – same address.)

Ludus, Owen House, 6 Thurnham Street, Lancaster LA1 1YD. Tel. 0524 35936–7.

Lynx Dance, c/o Lincolnshire & Humberside Arts, St Hugh's, Newport, Lincoln LN1 3DN. Tel. 0522 22555.

Mantis Dance Company, c/o Dance Umbrella Ltd., 10 Greek Street, London, W1V 5LE. Tel. 01-437 2617.

Midlands Dance Company (formerly EMMA Dance Company), United Reformed Church Hall, Frederick Street, Loughborough, Leics. Tel. 0509 2637.

Moving Being, St Stephen's Theatre Space, Cardiff, Tel. 0222 498885.

Nin Dance Company, c/o 6 Norcott Road, London. N16. Tel. 01-806 8089.

Second Stride, c/o Dance Umbrella Ltd., 10 Greek Street, London, W1V 5LE. Tel. 01-437 2617.

Spiral, 8 Sandyway, Birkenhead, Wirral, Merseyside L43 IT2. Tel. 051-724 4044.

3. SUGGESTED READING

General introduction

Richard Glasstone: *Male Dancing as a Career*. Kaye & Ward, London, 1980.

Louis Horst and Carroll Russell: *Modern Dance Forms*. Dance Horizons, New York, 1973 (paperback).

Joseph H. Mazo: *Prime Movers: The Makers of Modern Dance in America*. William Morrow & Co., New York, 1977.

Jan Murray: *Dance Now*. Penguin, Harmondsworth, 1977 (paperback).

Rudi van Dantzig: *Ballet and Modern Dance*. Octopus Books, London, 1974.

Ian Woodward: *Ballet*. Teach Yourself Books (Hodder & Stoughton), London, 1977 (paperback).

Ian Woodward: *Spotlight on Ballet*. Knight Books (Hodder & Stoughton), London, 1980 (paperback).

Dancers and choreographers

Isadora Duncan: *My Life* (autobiography). Gollancz, London, 1968.

Moira Hodgson: *Quintet: Five American Dance Companies* [Alvin Ailey, Merce Cunningham, Eliot Feld, Paul Taylor, Dance Theatre of Harlem]. Gage, New York, 1976.

James Klosty (editor): *Merce Cunningham*. E. P. Dutton & Co., New York, 1975 (paperback).

Don McDonagh: *Martha Graham: a biography*. David & Charles, London, 1974. Also in paperback: Popular Library, New York, 1975.

Olga Maynard: *American Modern Dancers: the Pioneers*. Little, Brown & Co., Boston, Toronto, 1965.

Joseph Mazo: *The Alvin Ailey American Dance Theatre*. William Morrow & Co., New York, 1978 (paperback).

Reference

Anatole Chujoy and P. W. Manchester: *The Dance Encyclopaedia*. Simon & Schuster, New York, 1967.

Mary Clarke and David Vaughan: *The Encyclopaedia of Dance and Ballet*. Pitman Publishing, London, 1977.

Horst Koegler: *The Concise Oxford Dictionary of Ballet*. Oxford University Press, London, 1977.

Don McDonagh: *Complete Guide to Modern Dance* [biographies of choreographers and background details of their works]. Popular Library, New York, 1977 (paperback).

New Dance, a quarterly magazine about improvisation and other modern dance forms. Published from 147 Knapp Road, London, E9.

If you've enjoyed this book, you may
also like to read some of the stories
about the theatre and ballet listed
on the next page:

Theatre and ballet stories available from Knight Books

Mary Denison

☐ 24880 7 AT MADAM MURIEL'S 85p

Susan Clement Farrar

☐ 26542 6 SAMANTHA ON STAGE 95p

Jean Richardson

☐ 24030 X THE FIRST STEP £1.10
☐ 26260 5 DANCER IN THE WINGS 95p
☐ 26813 1 ONE FOOT ON THE GROUND £1.10